ever EVER

increasing INCREASING

faith FAITH

ever increasing faith

Smith Wigglesworth

Whitaker House

EVER INCREASING FAITH

ISBN: 0-88368-633-3
Printed in the United States of America
© 2000 by Whitaker House

Whitaker House
30 Hunt Valley Circle
New Kensington, PA 15068

Library of Congress Cataloging-in-Publication Data

Wigglesworth, Smith, 1859–1947.
    Ever increasing faith / by Smith Wigglesworth.
        p. cm.
    ISBN 0-88368-633-3 (alk. paper)
    1. Spiritual life—Pentecostal churches. 2. Gifts,
    Spiritual—Pentecostal churches. I. Title.
BV3797 .W45 2000
234'.13—dc21   00-011671

Contents

Introduction

An encounter with Smith Wigglesworth was an unforgettable experience. This seems to be the universal reaction of all who knew him or heard him speak. Smith Wigglesworth was a simple yet remarkable man who was used in an extraordinary way by our extraordinary God. He had a contagious and inspiring faith. Under his ministry, thousands of people came to salvation, committed themselves to a deeper faith in Christ, received the baptism in the Holy Spirit, and were miraculously healed. The power that brought these kinds of results was the presence of the Holy Spirit, who filled Smith Wigglesworth and used him in bringing the good news of the Gospel to people all over the world. Wigglesworth gave glory to God for everything that was accomplished through his ministry, and he wanted people to understand his work only in this context, because his sole desire was that people would see Jesus and not himself.

Smith Wigglesworth was born in England in 1859. Immediately after his conversion as a boy, he had a concern for the salvation of others and won people to Christ, including his mother. Even so, as a young man, he could not express himself well enough to give a short testimony in church, much less preach a sermon. Wigglesworth said that his mother had the same difficulty in expressing herself that he did. This family trait, coupled with the fact that he had no formal education because he began working twelve hours a day at the age of seven to help support the family, contributed to Wigglesworth's awkward speaking style. He became a plumber by trade, yet he continued to devote himself to winning many people to Christ on an individual basis.

In 1882, he married Polly Featherstone, a vivacious young woman who loved God and had a gift of preaching and evangelism. It was she who taught him to read and who became his closest confidant and strongest supporter. They both had compassion for the poor and needy in their community, and they opened a mission, at which Polly preached. Significantly, people were miraculously healed when Wigglesworth prayed for them.

In 1907, Wigglesworth's circumstances changed dramatically when, at the age of forty-eight, he was baptized in the Holy Spirit. Suddenly, he had a new power that enabled him to preach, and even his wife was amazed at the transformation. This was the beginning of what became a worldwide evangelistic and healing ministry that reached thousands. He eventually ministered in the United States, Australia, South Africa, and all over Europe. His ministry extended up to the time of his death in 1947.

Several emphases in Smith Wigglesworth's life and ministry characterize him: a genuine, deep compassion for the unsaved and sick; an unflinching belief in the Word of God; a desire that Christ should increase and he should decrease (John 3:30); a belief that he was called to exhort people to enlarge their faith and trust in God;

an emphasis on the baptism in the Holy Spirit with the manifestation of the gifts of the Spirit as in the early church; and a belief in complete healing for everyone of all sickness.

Smith Wigglesworth was called "The Apostle of Faith" because absolute trust in God was a constant theme of both his life and his messages. In his meetings, he would quote passages from the Word of God and lead lively singing to help build people's faith and encourage them to act on it. He emphasized belief in the fact that God could do the impossible. He had great faith in what God could do, and God did great things through him.

Wigglesworth's unorthodox methods were often questioned. As a person, Wigglesworth was reportedly courteous, kind, and gentle. However, he became forceful when dealing with the devil, whom he believed caused all sickness. Wigglesworth said the reason he spoke bluntly and acted forcefully with people was that he knew he needed to get their attention so they could focus on God. He also had such anger toward the devil and sickness that he acted in a seemingly rough way. When he prayed for people to be healed, he would often hit or punch them at the place of their problem or illness. Yet no one was hurt by this startling treatment. Instead, they were remarkably healed. When he was asked why he treated people in this manner, he said that he was not hitting the people but that he was hitting the devil. He believed that the devil should never be treated gently or allowed to get away with anything. About twenty people were reportedly raised from the dead after he prayed for them. Wigglesworth himself was healed of appendicitis and kidney stones, after which his brusque personality softened, and he was more gentle with those who came to him for prayer for healing. His abrupt manner as he ministered may be attributed to the fact that he was very serious about his calling and got down to business quickly.

Although Wigglesworth believed in complete healing, he encountered illnesses and deaths that were difficult to understand. These included the deaths of his wife and son, his daughter's lifelong deafness, and his own battles with kidney stones and sciatica.

He often seemed paradoxical: compassionate but forceful, blunt but gentle, a well-dressed gentleman whose speech was often ungrammatical or confusing. However, he loved God with everything he had, he was steadfastly committed to God and to His Word, and he didn't rest until he saw God move in the lives of those who needed Him.

In 1936, Smith Wigglesworth prophesied about what we now know as the charismatic movement. He accurately predicted that the established mainline denominations would experience revival and the gifts of the Spirit in a way that would surpass even the Pentecostal movement. Wigglesworth did not live to see the renewal, but as an evangelist and a prophet with a remarkable healing ministry, he had a tremendous influence on both the Pentecostal and charismatic movements, and his example and influence on believers is felt to this day.

Without the power of God that was so obviously present in his life and ministry, we might not be reading transcripts of his sermons, for his spoken messages were often disjointed and ungrammatical. However, true gems of spiritual insight shine through them because of the revelation he received through the Holy Spirit. It was his life of complete devotion and belief in God and his reliance on the Holy Spirit that brought the life-changing power of God into his messages.

Introduction

Because of Wigglesworth's unique style, the messages in this book have been edited for clarity, and archaic expressions that would be unfamiliar to modern readers have been updated. At his meetings, he would often speak in tongues and give the interpretation, and these interpretations have been included with his messages.

In conclusion, we hope that as you read these words of Smith Wigglesworth, you will truly sense his complete trust and unwavering faith in God and take to heart one of his favorite sayings: "Only believe!"

I

Have Faith in God

For assuredly, I say to you, whoever says to this
mountain, "Be removed and be cast into the sea,"
and does not doubt in his heart, but believes
that those things he says will be done, he will have
whatever he says. Therefore I say to you, whatever things
you ask when you pray, believe that you receive them,
and you will have them.
—Mark 11:23–24

These are days when we need to have our faith strengthened, when we need to know God. God has designed that the just will live by faith (Rom. 1:17). Any man can be changed by faith, no matter how he may be fettered. I know that God's Word is sufficient. One word from Him can change a nation. His Word is *"from everlasting to everlasting"* (Ps. 90:2). It is through the entrance of this everlasting Word, this incorruptible seed, that we are born again and come into this wonderful salvation. *"Man shall not live by bread alone, but by every word that proceeds from the mouth of God"* (Matt. 4:4). This is the food of faith. *"Faith comes by hearing, and hearing by the word of God"* (Rom. 10:17).

EVER INCREASING FAITH

God's Word Is Sure

Everywhere men are trying to discredit the Bible and take from it all that is miraculous in it. One preacher says, "Well, you know, Jesus arranged beforehand to have that colt tied where it was and for the men to say just what they did." (See Matthew 21:2–3.)

I tell you, God can arrange everything. He can plan for you, and when He plans for you, all is peace. All things are possible if you will believe (Mark 9:23).

Another preacher says, "It was an easy thing for Jesus to feed the people with five loaves. The loaves were so big in those days that it was a simple matter to cut them into a thousand pieces each." (See John 6:5–13.) But he forgets that one little boy brought those five loaves all the way in his lunch basket.

Nothing is impossible with God. All the impossibility is with us when we measure God by the limitations of our unbelief.

Reaching Out in Faith

We have a wonderful God, a God whose ways are past finding out and whose grace and power are limitless. I was in Belfast one day and saw one of the brothers of the assembly. He said to me, "Wigglesworth, I am troubled. I have had a good deal of sorrow during the past five months. I had a woman in my assembly who could always pray the blessing of heaven down on our meetings. She is an old woman, yet her presence is always an inspiration. Five months ago she fell and broke her leg. The doctors put her into a plaster cast, and after five months, they broke the cast off. However, the bones were not properly set, and so she fell and broke her thighbone again."

He took me to her house, and there was a woman lying in a bed on the right-hand side of the room. I said to her, "Well, what about it now?"

She said, "They have sent me home incurable. The doctors say that I am so old that my bones won't knit. They say there is no nutriment in my bones, and they will never be able to do anything for me. They say I will have to lie in bed for the rest of my life."

I said to her, "Can you believe God?"

She replied, "Yes, ever since I heard that you had come to Belfast my faith has been quickened. If you will pray, I will believe. I know there is no power on earth that can make the bones of my leg knit, but I know there is nothing impossible with God."

I said, "Do you believe He will meet you now?"

She answered, "I do."

It is grand to see people believe God. God knew all about this leg and that it was broken in two places. I said to the woman, "When I pray, something will happen."

Her husband was sitting there; he had been in his chair for four years and could not walk a step. He called out, "I don't believe. I won't believe. You will never get me to believe."

I said, "All right," and laid my hands on his wife in the name of the Lord Jesus.

The moment hands were laid upon her, the power of God went right through her, and she cried out, "I'm healed."

I said, "I'm not going to assist you to rise. God will do it all." She arose and walked up and down the room, praising God.

The old man was amazed at what had happened to his wife, and he cried out, "Make me walk; make me walk."

I said to him, "You old sinner, repent."

He cried out, "Lord, you know I never meant what I said. Lord, You know I believe."

I don't think he meant what he said; the Lord was full of compassion anyway. If He marked our sins, where would any of us be? If we will meet the conditions, God will always meet us. If we believe, all things are possible.

I laid my hands on him, and the power went right through the old man's body. For the first time in four years, those legs received power to carry his body. He walked up and down and in and out of the room. He said, "Oh, what great things God has done for us tonight!"

"Whatever things you ask when you pray, believe that you receive them, and you will have them." Desire God, and you will have desires from God. He will meet you on the line of those desires when you reach out in simple faith.

A man came to me in one of my meetings who had seen other people healed and wanted to be healed, too. He explained that his arm had been set in a certain position for many years, and he could not move it. "Got any faith?" I asked.

He said that he had a lot of faith. After prayer he was able to swing his arm round and round. But he was not satisfied and complained, "I feel a little bit of trouble just there," pointing to a certain place.

I said, "Do you know what the trouble is with you?"

He answered, "No."

I said, "Imperfect faith." *"Whatever things you ask when you pray, believe that you receive them, and you will have them."*

Did you believe before you were saved? So many people want to be saved, but they want to feel saved first. There never was a man who felt saved before he believed. God's plan is always as follows: if you will believe, you will see the glory of God (John 11:40). I believe God wants to bring us all to a definite place of unswerving faith and confidence in Himself.

In our text from Mark, Jesus uses the illustration of a mountain. Why does He speak of a mountain? If faith can remove a mountain, it can remove anything. The plan of God is so marvelous that if you will only believe, all things are possible.

Love Has No Doubts

There is one special phrase from our text to which I want to call your attention: *"And does not doubt in his heart."* The heart is the mainspring. Imagine a young man and a young woman. They have fallen in love at first sight. In a short while there is a deep affection and a strong heart love, the one toward the other. What is a heart of love? It is a heart of faith. Faith and love are kin. In the measure that the young man and the young woman love one another, they are true. One may go to the North and the other to the South, but because of their love, they will be true to one another.

It is the same when there is a deep love in the heart toward the Lord Jesus Christ. In this new life into which God has brought us, Paul told us that we have become dead to the law by the body of Christ, so that we should be married to another, even to Him who is raised from the dead (Rom. 7:4). God brings us into a place of perfect love and perfect faith. A man who is born of God is brought into an inward affection, a loyalty to the Lord Jesus that shrinks from anything impure. You see the purity of a man and woman when there is a deep natural affection between them; they disdain the very thought of either of them being untrue. In the same way, in the measure that a man has faith in Jesus, he is pure. He who believes that Jesus is the Christ overcomes the world (1 John 5:5). It is a faith that works by love (Gal. 5:6).

Just as we have heart fellowship with our Lord, our faith cannot be daunted. We cannot doubt in our hearts. As we go on with God, there comes a wonderful association, an impartation of His very life and nature within. As we read His Word and believe the promises that He has so graciously given to us, we are made partakers of His very essence and life. The Lord is made a Bridegroom to us, and we are His bride. His words to us are spirit and life (John 6:63), transforming us and changing us, expelling what is natural and bringing in what is divine.

It is impossible to comprehend the love of God when we think along natural lines. We must have the revelation from the Spirit of God. God gives liberally. He who asks, receives (Matt. 7:8). God is willing to bestow on us all things that pertain to life and godliness (2 Pet. 1:3). Oh, it was the love of God that brought Jesus, and it is this same love that helps you and me to believe. God will be your strength in every weakness (2 Cor. 12:9–10). You who need His touch, remember that He loves you. If you are wretched, helpless, or sick, look to the God of all grace, whose very essence is love, who delights to give liberally all the inheritance of life and strength and power of which you are in need.

Be Cleansed Today

When I was in Switzerland, the Lord was graciously working and healing many of the people. I was staying with Brother Reuss of Goldiwil, and two policemen were sent to his home to arrest me. The charge was that I was healing the people without a license. Mr. Reuss said to them, "I am sorry that he is not here just now; he is holding a meeting about two miles away. But before you arrest him, I would like to show you something."

Brother Reuss took these two policemen down to one of the rougher parts of that district, to a house with which they were familiar, for they had often gone to that place to arrest a certain woman who was repeatedly an inmate of the prison because of continually being engaged in drunken brawls. He took them to this woman and said to them, "This is one of the many cases of blessing that have come through the ministry of the man you have come to arrest. This woman came to our meeting in a drunken condition. Her body was broken, for she was ruptured in two places. While she was drunk, the evangelist laid his hands on her and asked God to heal her and deliver her."

The woman joined in, "Yes, and God saved me, and I have not tasted a drop of liquor since."

The policemen had a prepared warrant for my arrest, but they said with disgust, "Let the doctors do this kind of thing." They turned and went away, and that was the last we heard of them.

We have a Jesus who heals the brokenhearted, who lets the captives go free, who saves the very worst. Do you dare spurn this glorious Gospel of God for spirit, soul, and body? Do you dare spurn this grace? I realize that this full Gospel has in great measure been hidden, this Gospel that brings liberty, this Gospel that brings souls out of bondage, this Gospel that brings perfect health to the body, this Gospel of entire salvation. Listen again to the words of Him who left glory to bring us this great salvation: *"Assuredly, I say to you, whoever says to this mountain, 'Be removed,'...he will have whatever he says."* Whatever!

I realize that God can never bless us when we are being hard-hearted, critical, or unforgiving. These things will hinder faith quicker than anything. I remember being at a meeting where there were some people waiting for the baptism and seeking for cleansing, for the moment a person is cleansed the Spirit will fall. There was one man who had red eyes from weeping bitterly. He said to me, "I will have to leave. It is no good my staying unless I change things. I have written a letter to my brother-in-law and filled it with hard words, and this thing must first be straightened out."

He went home and told his wife, "I'm going to write a letter to your brother and ask him to forgive me for writing to him the way I did."

"You fool!" she said.

"Never mind," he replied, "this thing is between God and me, and it has got to be cleared away." He wrote the letter and came again, and immediately God filled him with the Spirit.

I believe there are a great many people who want to be healed, but they are harboring things in their hearts that are like a blight. Let these things go. Forgive, and the Lord will forgive you. There are many good people, people who mean well, but they have no power to do anything for God. There is just some little thing that came in their hearts years ago, and their faith has been paralyzed ever since.

Bring everything to the light. God will sweep it all away if you will let Him. Let the precious blood of Christ cleanse you from all sin. If you will only believe, God will meet you and bring into your life the sunshine of His love.

Have Faith in God

Healings in New Zealand

We have received numerous testimonies of those healed in the meeting conducted by Brother Smith Wigglesworth at Wellington, New Zealand. Mrs. E. Curtis of Christchurch, New Zealand, was suffering with septic poisoning. She had become only a skeleton, and the doctors could do nothing for her. She had agonizing pains all day and all night. She was healed immediately when prayer was made for her. She states that for the past sixteen years, she has been a martyr to pain but is now wonderfully well.

Another testified to healing of deafness, goiter, adenoids, and bad eyesight. Another woman testified to healing of double curvature of the spine from infancy, hip disease, weak heart, and a leg lengthened three inches, which grew out normal like the other leg. It had been also three inches less in circumference. She had worn a large boot with a built-up sole, but now she walks on even-soled shoes, the large boot having been discarded. Another was healed of a goiter through an anointed handkerchief.

—from *The Pentecostal Evangel*

2

Deliverance to the Captives

Then Jesus, being filled with the Holy Spirit, returned from the Jordan and was led by the Spirit into the wilderness, being tempted for forty days by the devil. And in those days He ate nothing, and afterward, when they had ended, He was hungry. And the devil said to Him, "If You are the Son of God, command this stone to become bread." But Jesus answered him, saying, "It is written, 'Man shall not live by bread alone, but by every word of God.'" Then the devil, taking Him up on a high mountain, showed Him all the kingdoms of the world in a moment of time. And the devil said to Him, "All this authority I will give You, and their glory; for this has been delivered to me, and I give it to whomever I wish. Therefore, if You will worship before me, all will be Yours." And Jesus answered and said to him, "Get behind Me, Satan! For it is written, 'You shall worship the LORD your God, and Him only you shall serve.'" Then he brought Him to Jerusalem, set Him on the pinnacle of the temple, and said to Him, "If You are the Son of God, throw Yourself down from here. For it is written: 'He shall give His angels charge over you, to keep you,' and, 'In their hands they shall bear you up, lest you dash your foot against a stone.'" And Jesus answered and said to him,

EVER INCREASING FAITH

"It has been said, 'You shall not tempt the LORD your God'" Now when the devil had ended every temptation, he departed from Him until an opportune time. Then Jesus returned in the power of the Spirit to Galilee, and news of Him went out through all the surrounding region. And He taught in their synagogues, being glorified by all. So He came to Nazareth, where He had been brought up. And as His custom was, He went into the synagogue on the Sabbath day, and stood up to read. And He was handed the book of the prophet Isaiah. And when He had opened the book, He found the place where it was written: "The Spirit of the LORD is upon Me, because He has anointed Me to preach the gospel to the poor; He has sent Me to heal the brokenhearted, to proclaim liberty to the captives and recovery of sight to the blind, to set at liberty those who are oppressed; to proclaim the acceptable year of the LORD." Then He closed the book, and gave it back to the attendant and sat down. And the eyes of all who were in the synagogue were fixed on Him.
—Luke 4:1–20

Our precious Lord Jesus has everything for everybody. Forgiveness of sin, healing of diseases, and the fullness of the Spirit all come from one source—from the Lord Jesus Christ. Hear Him who is *"the same yesterday, today, and forever"* (Heb. 13:8) as He announces the purpose for which He came:

> *The Spirit of the LORD is upon Me, because He has anointed Me to preach the gospel to the poor; He has sent Me to heal the brokenhearted, to proclaim liberty to the captives and recovery of sight to the blind, to set at liberty those who are oppressed; to proclaim the acceptable year of the LORD.* (Luke 4:18–19)

24

Deliverance to the Captives

God's Power Is Available to You

Jesus was baptized by John in the Jordan, and the Holy Spirit descended upon Him in a bodily shape like a dove. Being full of the Holy Spirit, He was led by the Spirit into the wilderness, there to emerge more than a conqueror over the archenemy. Then He returned *"in the power of the Spirit to Galilee"* and preached in the synagogues. At last He came to His old hometown, Nazareth, where He announced His mission in the words I have just quoted from Luke 4:18–19. For a brief while, He ministered on the earth, and then He gave His life a ransom for all. But God raised Him from the dead.

Before Jesus went to heaven, He told His disciples that they would receive the power of the Holy Spirit upon them, too (Acts 1:8). Thus, through them, His gracious ministry would continue. This power of the Holy Spirit was not only for a few apostles, but even for those who were afar off, even as many as our God would call (Acts 2:39), even for us way down in this century. Some ask, "But wasn't this power just for the privileged few in the first century?" No. Read the Master's Great Commission as recorded in Mark 16:15–18, and you will see it is for those who believe.

The Purpose of the Power

After I received the baptism in the Holy Spirit—and I know that I received it, for the Lord gave me the Spirit in just the same way that He gave Him to the disciples at Jerusalem—I sought the mind of the Lord as to why I had been baptized. One day I came home from work and went into the house, and my wife asked me, "Which way did you come in?" I told her that I had come in by the back door. She said, "There is a woman upstairs, and she has brought an eighty-year-old man to be prayed for. He is raving up there, and a great crowd has gathered outside the front door, ringing the doorbell and wanting to know what is going on in the house."

The Lord quietly whispered, "This is what I baptized you for."

I carefully opened the door of the room where the man was, desiring to be obedient to what my Lord would say to me. The man was crying and shouting in distress, "I am lost! I am lost! I have committed the unpardonable sin. I am lost! I am lost!"

My wife asked, "Smith, what should we do?"

The Spirit of the Lord moved me to cry out, "Come out, you lying spirit." In a moment the evil spirit went, and the man was free. God gives deliverance to the captives!

And the Lord said again to me, "This is what I baptized you for."

There is a place where God, through the power of the Holy Spirit, reigns supreme in our lives. The Spirit reveals, unfolds, takes of the things of Christ and shows them to us (John 16:15), and prepares us to be more than a match for satanic forces.

Miracles Are for Today

When Nicodemus came to Jesus, he said, *"Rabbi, we know that You are a teacher come from God; for no one can do these signs that You do unless God is with him"* (John 3:2). Jesus replied, *"Most assuredly, I say to you, unless one is born again, he cannot see the kingdom of God"* (v. 3).

Nicodemus was impressed by Jesus' miracles, and Jesus pointed out to him the necessity of a miracle being done in every man who would see the kingdom. When a man is born of God—is brought from darkness to light—a mighty miracle is performed. Jesus saw every touch of God as a miracle, and so we may expect to see miracles today. It is wonderful to have the Spirit of the Lord upon us. I would rather have the Spirit of God on me for five minutes than receive a million dollars.

The Antidote for Unbelief

Do you see how Jesus mastered the devil in the wilderness? (See Luke 4:1–14.) Jesus knew He was the Son of God, and the devil came along with an "if." How many times has the enemy come along to you this way? He says, "After all, you may be deceived. You know you really are not a child of God." If the devil comes along and says that you are not saved, it is a pretty sure sign that you are. When he comes and tells you that you are not healed, it may be taken as good evidence that the Lord has sent His Word and healed you (Ps. 107:20). Satan knows that if he can capture your thought life, he has won a mighty victory over you. His great business is injecting thoughts, but if you are pure and holy, you will instantly shrink from them. God wants us to let the mind that was in Christ Jesus, that pure, holy, humble mind of Christ, be in us (Phil. 2:5).

I come across people everywhere I go who are held bound by deceptive conditions, and these conditions have come about simply because they have allowed the devil to make their minds the place of his stronghold. How are we to guard against this? The Lord has provided us with weapons that are mighty through God for the pulling down of these strongholds of the enemy (2 Cor. 10:4), by means of which every thought will be brought *"into captivity to the obedience of Christ"* (v. 5). Jesus' blood and His mighty name are an antidote to all the subtle seeds of unbelief that the devil would sow in your mind.

Christ's Amazing Works Today

In the first chapter of Acts, we see that Jesus commanded the disciples to *"wait for the Promise of the Father"* (v. 4). He told them that not many days from then they would be baptized in the Holy Spirit (v. 5). Luke told us that he had written his former account concerning *"all that Jesus began both to do and teach"* (v. 1). The ministry of Christ did not end at the Cross, but the book of Acts and the Epistles give us accounts of what He continued to do and teach through those whom He indwelt.

Our blessed Lord Jesus is still alive and still continues His ministry through those who are filled with His Spirit. He is still healing the brokenhearted and delivering the captives through those on whom He places His Spirit.

I was traveling one day on a railway train in Sweden. At one station, an old lady boarded the train with her daughter. That old lady's expression was so troubled that I inquired what was the matter with her. I heard that she was going to the hospital to have her leg amputated. She began to weep as she told me that the doctors had said that there was no hope for her except through having her leg amputated. She was seventy years old. I said to my interpreter, "Tell her that Jesus can heal her." The instant my interpreter said this to her, her face became so radiant that it was as if a heavy veil had been removed.

We stopped at another station, and the railway car filled up with people. A large group of men rushed to board the train, and the devil said, "You're done." But I knew I had the best position, because hard things are always opportunities to gain more glory for the Lord as He manifests His power.

Every trial is a blessing. There have been times when I have been hard-pressed through dire circumstances, and it seemed as if a dozen steamrollers were going over me, but I have found that the hardest things are just lifting places into the grace of God. We have such a lovely Jesus. He always proves Himself to be such a mighty Deliverer. He never fails to plan the best things for us.

The train began moving, and I crouched down and in the name of Jesus commanded the disease to leave. The old lady cried, "I'm healed! I know I'm healed!" She stamped her leg and said, "I'm going to prove it." So when we stopped at another station, she marched up and down and shouted, "I'm not going to the hospital." Once again our wonderful Jesus had proven Himself a Healer of the brokenhearted, a Deliverer of one who was bound.

My Own Remarkable Healing

At one time I was so bound that no human power could help me. My wife thought that I would pass away. There was no help. At that time I had just had a faint glimpse of Jesus as the Healer. For six months I had been suffering from appendicitis, occasionally getting temporary relief. I went to the mission of which I was the pastor, but I was brought to the floor in awful agony, and I was brought home to my bed. All night I was praying, pleading for deliverance, but none came.

My wife was sure it was my call home to heaven and sent for a physician. The doctor said that there was no possible chance for me—my body was too weak. Having had the appendicitis for six months, my whole system was drained, and, because of that, he thought that it was too late for an operation. He left my wife in a state of brokenheartedness.

After he left, a young man and an old lady came to our door. I knew that the old lady was a woman of real prayer. They came upstairs to my room. This young man jumped on the bed and commanded the evil spirit to come out of me. He shouted, "Come out, you devil! I command you to come out in the name of Jesus!" There was no chance for an argument or for me to tell him that I would never believe that there was a devil inside of me. The thing had to go in the name of Jesus, and it went. I was instantly healed.

I arose and dressed and went downstairs. I was still in the plumbing business, and I asked my wife, "Is there any work in? I'm all right now, and I am going to work." I found that there was a certain job to be done, and so I picked up my tools and went off to do it.

Just after I left, the doctor came in, put his hat down in the hall, and walked up to the bedroom. But the invalid was not there. "Where is Mr. Wigglesworth?" he asked.

"Oh, doctor, he's gone out to work," said my wife.

"You'll never see him alive again," said the doctor. "They'll bring him back a corpse."

Well, you see before you the corpse.

Since that time, in many parts of the world, the Lord has given me the privilege of praying for people with appendicitis; and I have personally witnessed a great many people up and dressed within a quarter of an hour from the time I prayed for them. We have a living Christ who is willing to meet people in every place.

A Man Whose Bride Was Dying

A number of years ago I met Brother D. W. Kerr, and he gave me a letter of introduction to a brother in Zion City named Cook. I took his letter to Brother Cook, and he said, "God has sent you here." He gave me the addresses of six people and asked me to go and pray for them and meet him again at twelve o'clock.

I got back at about 12:30, and he told me about a young man who was to be married the following Monday. His sweetheart was dying of appendicitis. I went to the house and found that the physician had just been there and had pronounced that there was no hope. The mother was distraught and was pulling her hair and saying, "Is there no deliverance?"

I said to her, "Woman, believe God, and your daughter will be healed and be up and dressed in fifteen minutes." But the mother went on screaming.

They took me into the bedroom, and I prayed for the girl and commanded the evil spirit to depart in the name of Jesus. She cried, "I am healed."

I said to her, "Do you want me to believe that you are healed? If you are healed, get up."

She said, "You get out of the room, and I'll get up." In less than ten minutes, the doctor came in. He wanted to know what had happened. She said, "A man came in and prayed for me, and I am healed."

The doctor pressed his finger right in the place that had been so sore, and the girl neither moaned nor cried. He said, "This is God." It made no difference whether he acknowledged it or not; I knew that God had worked.

Our God is real, and He has saving and healing power today. Our Jesus is just the same *"yesterday, today, and forever"* (Heb. 13:8). He saves and heals today just as of old, and He wants to be your Savior and your Healer.

Oh, if you would only believe God! What would happen? The greatest things.

Some have never tasted the grace of God, have never had the peace of God. Unbelief robs them of these blessings. It is possible to hear and yet not perceive the truth. It is possible to read the Word and not share in the life it brings. It is necessary for us to have the Holy Spirit to unfold the Word and bring to us the life that is Christ. We can never fully understand the wonders of this redemption until we are full of the Holy Spirit.

Disease Due to Immorality

One time I was at an afternoon meeting. The Lord had been graciously with us, and many had been healed by the power of God. Most of the people had gone home when I saw a young man who evidently was hanging back to have a word with me. I asked, "What do you want?"

He said, "I wonder if I could ask you to pray for me."

I said, "What's the trouble?"

He said, "Can't you smell?" The young man had gone into sin and was suffering the consequences. He said, "I have been turned out of two hospitals. I am broken out all over. I have abscesses all over me." I could see that he was badly broken out on his nose. He said, "I heard you preach and could not understand about this healing business, and I was wondering if there was any hope for me."

I asked him, "Do you know Jesus?" He did not know the first thing about salvation, but I said to him,

"Stand still." I placed my hands on him and cursed that terrible disease in the name of Jesus.

He cried out, "I know I'm healed. I can feel a warmth and a glow all over me."

I said, "Who did it?"

He said, "Your prayers."

I said, "No, it was Jesus!"

He said, "Was it He? Oh, Jesus! Jesus! Jesus, save me." And that young man went away healed and saved. Oh, what a merciful God we have! What a wonderful Jesus is ours!

A Place of Deliverance

Are you oppressed? Cry out to God. It is always good for people to cry out to the Lord. You may have to cry out. The Holy Spirit and the Word of God will bring to light every hidden, unclean thing that must be revealed. There is always a place of deliverance when you let God search out whatever is spoiling and marring your life.

The evil spirit that was in the man in the synagogue cried out, *"Let us alone!"* (Mark 1:24). It is notable that the evil spirit never cried out like that until Jesus walked into the place where he was. Jesus rebuked the thing, saying, *"Be quiet, and come out of him!"* (v. 25), and the man was delivered. He is just the same Jesus, exposing the powers of evil, delivering the captives and letting the oppressed go free, purifying them and cleansing their hearts.

The evil spirits that inhabited the man who had the legion did not want to be sent to the pit to be tormented before their time, and so they cried out to be sent into the swine. (See Luke 8:27–35.) Hell is such an awful place that even the demons hate the thought of going there. How much more should men seek to be saved from the pit?

God is compassionate and says, *"Seek the LORD while He may be found"* (Isa. 55:6). He has further stated, *"Whoever calls on the name of the LORD shall be saved"* (Acts 2:21). Seek Him now; call on His name right now. There is forgiveness, healing, redemption, deliverance—everything you need right here and now, and that which will satisfy you throughout eternity.

❧ ⊱—⊰ ☙

Blessings in Australia

By Sister Winnie Andrews, N. Melbourne, Australia

Our Brother Wigglesworth landed here February 16th, and had a meeting that very night. The dear Lord was present and that to heal. A little girl of six, having never walked, after she had been prayed for, walked out of the front door with her mother, who was full of joy for what the Lord had done for her little one. Another man, who had been suffering with bad feet for years and walked only with the aid of a stick, was instantly healed and has been along several times to testify to what the Lord has done for him. Many deaf people have been delivered in answer to the prayer of faith.

One night a dear man and his wife, whom he brought to the meeting in a wheelchair, were both healed. He had been suffering from deafness for twenty years, and she had not walked for over six-and-a-half years. After prayer, she got out of her chair and walked to the station, with her husband pushing the empty chair. He, too, was rejoicing in that he was now able to hear perfectly. O what a wonderful God we have. Blessed be His holy name!

At the Sunday afternoon service, a dear young woman who had been suffering with tuberculosis for thirteen years and who was in the last stages, came leaning on the arm of a friend and was prayed for. At once she received new life and was perfectly delivered. The terrible burning sores, which were eating their way into her bones, have dried up and are peeling off, and she is looking so well and happy and is as strong as can be. Glory to God!

Last night a young man suffering from consumption was prayed for and was instantly made whole. Oh, our hearts overflow at the glorious things God is doing in our midst!

Many have been healed of neuritis, heart and lung trouble, and stiff joints. One woman who had not walked for twenty-two years and could not as much as turn her head—after prayer—got out of bed and walked. Praise God!

—*The Pentecostal Evangel,* 15 April 1922

3

The Power of the Name

*Now Peter and John went up together to the temple at the
hour of prayer, the ninth hour. And a certain man lame from
his mother's womb was carried, whom they laid daily at the
gate of the temple which is called Beautiful, to ask alms
from those who entered the temple; who, seeing Peter and
John about to go into the temple, asked for alms. And fixing
his eyes on him, with John, Peter said, "Look at us." So he
gave them his attention, expecting to receive something from
them. Then Peter said, "Silver and gold I do not have, but
what I do have I give you: In the name of Jesus Christ of
Nazareth, rise up and walk." And he took him by the right
hand and lifted him up, and immediately his feet and ankle
bones received strength. So he, leaping up, stood and walked
and entered the temple with them; walking, leaping, and
praising God. And all the people saw him walking and
praising God. Then they knew that it was he who sat
begging alms at the Beautiful Gate of the temple; and they
were filled with wonder and amazement at what had
happened to him. Now as the lame man who was healed
held on to Peter and John, all the people ran together to them
in the porch which is called Solomon's, greatly amazed. So
when Peter saw it, he responded to the people: "Men of
Israel, why do you marvel at this? Or why look so intently at
us, as though by our own power or godliness we had made*

this man walk? The God of Abraham, Isaac, and Jacob, the God of our fathers, glorified His Servant Jesus, whom you delivered up and denied in the presence of Pilate, when he was determined to let Him go. But you denied the Holy One and the Just, and asked for a murderer to be granted to you, and killed the Prince of life, whom God raised from the dead, of which we are witnesses. And His name, through faith in His name, has made this man strong, whom you see and know. Yes, the faith which comes through Him has given him this perfect soundness in the presence of you all."
—Acts 3:1–16

All things are possible through the name of Jesus (Matt. 19:26). *"God also has highly exalted Him and given Him the name which is above every name, that at the name of Jesus every knee should bow"* (Phil. 2:9–10). There is power to overcome everything in the world through the name of Jesus. I am looking forward to a wonderful union through the name of Jesus. *"There is no other name under heaven given among men by which we must be saved"* (Acts 4:12).

Speaking the Name of Jesus

I want to instill in you a sense of the power, the virtue, and the glory of that name. Six people went into the house of a sick man to pray for him. He was a leader in the Episcopal Church, and he lay in his bed utterly helpless, without even strength to help himself. He had read a little tract about healing and had heard about people praying for the sick. So he sent for these friends, who, he thought, could pray *"the prayer of faith"* (James 5:15). He was anointed according to James 5:14, but because he had no immediate manifestation of healing, he wept bitterly. The six people walked out of the room, somewhat crestfallen to see the man lying there in an unchanged condition.

When they were outside, one of the six said, "There is one thing we could have done. I wish you would all go back with me and try it." They all went back and got together in a group. This brother said, "Let us whisper the name of Jesus." At first, when they whispered this worthy name, nothing seemed to happen. But as they continued to whisper "Jesus! Jesus! Jesus!" the power began to fall. When they saw that God was beginning to work, their faith and joy increased, and they whispered the name louder and louder. As they did so, the man rose from his bed and dressed himself. The secret was just this: those six people had gotten their eyes off the sick man and were taken up with the Lord Jesus Himself. Their faith grasped the power in His name. Oh, if people would only appreciate the power in this name, there is no telling what would happen.

I know that through His name and through the power of His name we have access to God. The very face of Jesus fills the whole place with glory. All over the world there are people magnifying that name, and oh, what a joy it is for me to utter it.

Raising Lazarus

One day I went up into the mountains to pray. I had a wonderful day. I was on one of the high mountains of Wales. I had heard of one man going up onto this mountain to pray and the Spirit of the Lord meeting him so wonderfully that his face shone like that of an angel when he returned. Everyone in the village was talking about it. As I went up onto this mountain and spent the day in the presence of the Lord, His wonderful power seemed to envelop and saturate and fill me.

Two years before this time, there had come to our house two lads from Wales. They were just ordinary lads, but they became very zealous for God. They came to our mission and saw some of the works of God. They said to me, "We would not be surprised if the Lord brings you down to Wales to raise our Lazarus." They explained that the leader of their church was a man who had spent his days working in a tin mine and his nights preaching, and the result was that he had collapsed and contracted tuberculosis. For four years he had been a helpless invalid, having to be fed with a spoon.

When I was up on that mountaintop, I was reminded of the Transfiguration (see Matthew 17:1–8), and I felt that the Lord's only purpose in taking us into the glory is to prepare us for greater usefulness in the valley.

Interpretation of Tongues
The living God has chosen us for His divine inheritance, and He it is who is preparing us for our ministry, that it may be of God and not of man.

As I was on the mountaintop that day, the Lord said to me, "I want you to go and raise Lazarus."

I told the brother who had accompanied me about this, and when we got down to the valley, I wrote a postcard. It read, "When I was up on the mountain praying today, God told me that I was to go and raise Lazarus." I addressed the postcard to the man whose name had been given to me by the two lads.

When we arrived at the place, we went to the man to whom I had addressed the postcard. He looked at me and asked, "Did you send this?"

"Yes," I replied.

He said, "Do you think we believe in this? Here, take it." And he threw it at me.

The man called a servant and said, "Take this man and show him Lazarus." Then he said to me, "The moment you see him, you will be ready to go home. Nothing will keep you here." And everything he said was true from the natural standpoint. The man was helpless. He was nothing but a mass of bones with skin stretched over them. There was no life to be seen. Everything in him spoke of decay.

I said to him, "Will you shout? You remember that at Jericho the people shouted while the walls were still up. God has a similar victory for you if you will only believe." But I could not get him to believe. There was not an atom of faith there. He had made up his mind not to have anything.

It is a blessed thing to learn that God's Word can never fail. Never listen to human plans. God can work mightily when you persist in believing Him in spite of discouragement from the human standpoint. When I got back to the man to whom I had sent the postcard, he asked, "Are you ready to go now?"

I am not moved by what I see. I am moved only by what I believe. I know this: no man looks at the circumstances if he believes. No man relies on his feelings if he believes. The man who believes God has his request. Every man who comes into the Pentecostal condition can laugh at all things and believe God.

There is something in the Pentecostal work that is different from anything else in the world. Somehow, in Pentecost you know that God is a reality. Wherever the Holy Spirit has the right-of-way, the gifts of the Spirit will be in manifestation. Where these gifts are never in manifestation, I question whether He is present. Pentecostal people are spoiled for anything other than Pentecostal meetings. We want none of the entertainments that other churches are offering. When God comes in, He entertains us Himself. We are entertained by the King of Kings and Lord of Lords! Oh, it is wonderful.

There were difficult conditions in that Welsh village, and it seemed impossible to get the people to believe. "Ready to go home?" I was asked. But a man and a woman there asked us to come and stay with them.

I said to the people, "I want to know how many of you people can pray." No one wanted to pray. I asked if I could get seven people to pray with me for the poor man's deliverance. I said to the two people we were to stay with, "I will count on you two, and there is my friend and myself. We need three others." I told the people I trusted that some of them would awaken to their privilege and come in the morning and join us in prayer for the raising of Lazarus. It will never do to give way to human opinions. If God says a thing, you are to believe it.

I told the people that I would not eat anything that night. When I got to bed, it seemed as if the devil tried to place on me everything that he had placed on that poor man on the sickbed. When I awoke in the middle of the night, I had a cough and all the weakness of a man with tuberculosis. I rolled out of bed onto the floor and cried out to God to deliver me from the power of the devil. I shouted loud enough to wake everybody in the house, but nobody was disturbed. God gave the victory, and I got back into bed again as free as I had ever been in my life. At five o'clock the Lord awakened me and said to me, "Don't break bread until you break it around My table." At six o'clock He gave me these words: *"And I will raise him up"* (John 6:40).

I elbowed the fellow who was sleeping in the same room. He said, "Ugh!" I elbowed him again and said, "Do you hear? The Lord says He will raise him up."

At eight o'clock they said to me, "Have a little refreshment." But I have found prayer and fasting the greatest joy, and you will always find it so when you are led by God.

When we went to the house where Lazarus lived, there were eight of us altogether. No one can prove to me that God does not always answer prayer. He always does more than that. He always gives *"exceedingly abundantly above all that we ask or think"* (Eph. 3:20).

I will never forget how the power of God fell on us as we went into that sick man's room. Oh, it was lovely! As we made a circle around the bed, I got one brother to hold the sick man's hand on one side, and I held the other, and we each held the hand of the person next to us. I said, "We are not going to pray; we are just going to use the name of Jesus."

We all knelt down and whispered that one word, "Jesus! Jesus! Jesus!" The power of God fell, and then it lifted. Five times the power of God fell, and then it remained. But the man in the bed was unmoved.

Two years previously, someone had come along and had tried to raise him up, and the devil had used his lack of success as a means of discouraging Lazarus. I said, "I don't care what the devil says. If God says He will raise you up, it must be so. Forget everything else except what God says about Jesus."

A sixth time the power fell, and the sick man's lips began moving, and the tears began to fall. I said to him, "The power of God is here; it is yours to accept."

He said, "I have been bitter in my heart, and I know I have grieved the Spirit of God. Here I am, helpless. I cannot lift my hands or even lift a spoon to my mouth."

I said, "Repent, and God will hear you."

He repented and cried out, "O God, let this be to Your glory." As he said this, the power of the Lord went right through him.

I have asked the Lord never to let me tell this story except the way it happened, for I realize that God can never bless exaggerations. As we again said, "Jesus! Jesus! Jesus!" the bed shook, and the man shook.

I said to the people who were with me, "You can all go downstairs now. This is all God. I'm not going to assist him." I sat and watched that man get up and dress himself. We sang the doxology as he walked down the steps. I said to him, "Now, go tell what has happened."

The news soon spread everywhere that Lazarus had been raised up. People came from Llanelly and the surrounding district to see him and to hear his testimony. God brought salvation to many. Right out in the open air, this man told what God had done, and as a result, many were convicted and converted. All this occurred through the name of Jesus, *"through faith in His name"* (Acts 3:16). Yes, the faith that is by Him gave this sick man perfect soundness in the presence of them all.

A Lame Man Healed

In the passage from the third chapter of Acts, we read that Peter and John were helpless and uneducated. They had no college education. Nevertheless, they had been with Jesus. To them had come a wonderful revelation of the power of the name of Jesus. They had handed out the bread and fish after Jesus had multiplied them. They had sat at the table with Him, and John had often gazed into His face. Jesus often had had to rebuke

Peter, but He had manifested His love to him through it all. Yes, He loved Peter, the wayward one.

Oh, He's a loving Savior! I have been wayward and stubborn. I had an unmanageable temper at one time, but how patient He has been. I am here to tell you that there is power in Jesus and in His wondrous name to transform anyone, to heal anyone.

If only you will see Him as God's Lamb, as God's beloved Son, upon whom was laid *"the iniquity of us all"* (Isa. 53:6). If only you will see that Jesus paid the whole price for our redemption so that we might be free. Then you can enter into your purchased inheritance of salvation, of life, and of power.

Poor Peter and John! They had no money. But they had faith; they had the power of the Holy Spirit; they had God. You can have God even though you have nothing else. Even if you have lost your character, you can have God. I have seen the worst men saved by the power of God.

Dealing with a Potential Murderer

I was preaching one day about the name of Jesus, and there was a man leaning against a lamppost, listening. He needed the lamppost to enable him to stay on his feet. We had finished our open-air meeting, and the man was still leaning against the lamppost. I asked him, "Are you sick?" He showed me his hand, and I saw that he held a silver-handled dagger inside his coat. He told me that he had been on his way to kill his unfaithful wife, but that he had heard me speaking about the power of the name of Jesus and could not get away. He said that he felt just helpless. I said, "Kneel down." There on the square, with people passing back and forth, he got saved.

I took him to my home and clothed him with a new suit. I saw that there was something in that man that God could use. He said to me the next morning, "God has revealed Jesus to me. I see that all has been laid upon Jesus." I lent him some money, and he soon got together a wonderful little home. His faithless wife was living with another man, but he invited her back to the home that he had prepared for her. She came. Where enmity and hatred had been before, the whole situation was transformed by love. God made that man a minister wherever he went.

Everywhere there is power in the name of Jesus. God can *"save to the uttermost"* (Heb. 7:25).

An "Incurable" Man Healed

There comes to mind a meeting we had in Stockholm that I will always remember. There was a home for incurables there, and one of the patients was brought to the meeting. He had palsy and was shaking all over. He stood up in front of three thousand people and came to the platform, supported by two others. The power of God fell on him as I anointed him in the name of Jesus. The moment I touched him, he dropped his crutches and began to walk in the name of Jesus. He walked down the steps and around that great building in view of all the people. There is nothing that our God cannot do. He will do everything if you will dare to believe.

Someone said to me, "Will you go to this home for incurables?" They took me there on my rest day. They brought out the sick people into a great corridor, and in one hour the Lord set about twenty of them free.

The name of Jesus is so marvelous. Peter and John had no conception of all that was in that name; neither had the man who had been lame from his mother's womb, who was laid daily at the gate. But they had faith to say, *"In the name of Jesus Christ of Nazareth, rise up and walk"* (Acts 3:6). And as Peter *"took him by the right hand and lifted him up,...immediately his feet and ankle bones received strength"* (v. 7), and he went into the temple with them, walking and leaping and praising God. God wants you to see more of this sort of thing done. How can it be done? Through *"His name, through faith in His name"* (v. 16); through faith that is by Him.

᷂᷂᷂᷂᷂᷂᷃

Revivals in Scandinavia

By Anna Lewini

The writer had the privilege for three months one year of being in the center of Mr. Smith Wigglesworth's meetings in both Sweden and Denmark. It was a time of visitation from on high. I estimate that hundreds of people received Jesus as their Savior; thousands were healed from all kinds of diseases; also thousands of believers awoke to a new kind of life; and many, many received the baptism of the Holy Spirit as on the Day of Pentecost. For all this we give glory to Jesus. Here are a few examples of miracles my eyes have seen.

It was in Orebro, Sweden, where at that time there was held a Pentecostal Convention. I came to seek help myself, being worn out with long, unbroken service in the Lord's work. The next day there was a meeting for healing. After the preaching service, I went forward into the other hall, and I was surprised to find a crowd following in a few minutes. The hall was soon full with hundreds of men and women patiently waiting for a touch from God through His servant. Glory to God, we were not disappointed. As hands were laid upon me, the power of God went through me in a mighty way. I was immediately well.

It was wonderful to notice, as the ministry continued, the effect upon the people as the power of God came over them. Some lifted their hands, crying, "I am healed! I am healed!" Some fell on the platform under the power of the Spirit, having to be helped down. Others walked away as in a dream; others as if drunk with new wine, lost to everything but God; but all had faces transfigured with the glory of the Lord and magnifying Jesus. A young blind girl, as she was ministered to, cried out, "Oh, how many windows there are in this hall!" During the three weeks the meetings continued, the great chapel was crowded daily, multitudes being healed, and many saved. The testimony meetings were wonderful. One said, "I was deaf, they prayed, and Jesus healed me." Another, "I had consumption, and I am free." And so on.

At Skofde, in the smaller hall, set apart for those seeking the baptism of the Holy Spirit, I shall never forget the sight, how the people with eyes closed and hearts uplifted to God waited. Did the Holy Spirit fall on them? Of course, He did. Here also many were healed. At another place there was a young man whose body was spoiled because of sin, but the Lord is merciful with sinners. He was anointed, and when hands were laid on, the power of God went mightily over him. He said, "I am healed," but being broken down as a little child, confessing his sin; at the same moment the Lord saved him. Glory to God! He went into the large hall and testified to salvation and healing.

At Stockholm, long lines waited for hours to get in. The hall held eighteen hundred people. At nearly every meeting, crowds were unable to enter the building, but they waited on, often hours and hours, for the chance, if any left the building, to step into the place. Here was a man with two crutches, his whole body shaking with palsy, as he was lifted onto the platform. (Behind him five or six hundred more were waiting for help.) This man was anointed and hands were laid on him in the name of Jesus. He was still shaking. Then he dropped one crutch, and after a short time the other one. His body was still shaking, but he took the first step out *in faith*. Would it be? He lifted one foot and then the other, walked around the platform. The onlookers rejoiced with him. Then he walked around the auditorium. Hallelujah!

During the meeting a woman began to shout and shout. The preacher told her to be quiet, but instead she jumped up on a chair, flourishing her arms about and crying, "I am healed! I am healed! I had cancer in my mouth, and I was unsaved; but during the meeting, as I listened to the Word of God, the Lord saved me and healed me of cancer in my mouth." She shouted again, "I am saved! I am healed of cancer!" She was quite beside herself. The people laughed and cried together.

Here was another woman unable to walk, sitting in a chair as she was ministered to. Her experience was the same as hundreds of others. She rose up, looking around and wondering if, after all, it was a dream. Suddenly she laughed and said, "My leg is healed." Afterward, she said, "I am not saved," and streams of tears ran down her face. They prayed for her, and later she left the meeting, healed and saved and full of joy. We have a wonderful Savior. Glory to His holy name!

Out of many miracles in Norway, I quote two taken from Pastor Barratt's paper, *Korsets Seir* (The Victory of the Cross). A man and his son came in a taxi to the meeting. Both had crutches. The father had been in bed for two years and was unable to put his leg on the ground. He was ministered to first. He dropped both crutches, walking and praising God. When the son saw this, he cried out, "Help me, too," and after a little while the father and the son, without crutches and without a taxi, walked away from the hall together. The Word again is manifested; the same Jesus, the wonder-working Jesus, is just the same today.

Now Copenhagen, my homeland! During three weeks, thousands daily attended the meetings. Each morning two or three hundred were ministered to for healing. Each evening the platform was surrounded. Again and again, as each throng retired, another company came forward seeking salvation. Here many were baptized in the Holy Spirit. The testimony meetings were wonderful.

Now I will close with a vision given to a brother who attended these meetings. He was lost in intercession for the hundreds of sick waiting to be ministered to for healing. He saw an opening from the platform, where the sick were, right into glory. He saw wonderful beings in the form of men resting, who looked on with interest. Again he looked at the platform and saw a heavenly Being clothed in white, who all the time was more active than any other in helping the sick, and when *He* touched them, the effect was wonderful. Bent forms were made straight, their eyes shone, and they began to glorify and praise the Lord. A Voice said, "Healings are the smallest of the gifts; it is but a drop in the bucket in view of what God has in store for His children. You shall do greater works than these."   —from *Confidence*

4

"Do You Want to Be Made Well?"

After this there was a feast of the Jews, and Jesus went up to Jerusalem. Now there is in Jerusalem by the Sheep Gate a pool, which is called in Hebrew, Bethesda, having five porches. In these lay a great multitude of sick people, blind, lame, paralyzed, waiting for the moving of the water. For an angel went down at a certain time into the pool and stirred up the water; then whoever stepped in first, after the stirring of the water, was made well of whatever disease he had. Now a certain man was there who had an infirmity thirty-eight years. When Jesus saw him lying there, and knew that he already had been in that condition a long time, He said to him, "Do you want to be made well?" The sick man answered Him, "Sir, I have no man to put me into the pool when the water is stirred up; but while I am coming, another steps down before me." Jesus said to him, "Rise, take up your bed and walk." And immediately the man was made well, took up his bed, and walked. And that day was the Sabbath. The Jews therefore said to him who was cured, "It is the Sabbath; it is not lawful for you to carry your bed." He answered them, "He who made me well said to me, 'Take up your bed and walk'" Then they asked him, "Who is the Man who said to you, 'Take up your bed and walk'?" But the one

51

*who was healed did not know who it was, for Jesus
had withdrawn, a multitude being in that place.
Afterward Jesus found him in the temple, and said
to him, "See, you have been made well. Sin no more, lest
a worse thing come upon you." The man departed and
told the Jews that it was Jesus who had made him well.
For this reason the Jews persecuted Jesus, and sought to
kill Him, because He had done these things on the Sabbath.
But Jesus answered them, "My Father has been working
until now, and I have been working." Therefore the Jews
sought all the more to kill Him, because He not only broke
the Sabbath, but also said that God was His Father,
making Himself equal with God. Then Jesus answered
and said to them, "Most assuredly, I say to you, the Son
can do nothing of Himself, but what He sees the Father
do; for whatever He does, the Son also does in like manner.
For the Father loves the Son, and shows Him all things
that He Himself does; and He will show Him greater
works than these, that you may marvel. For as the Father
raises the dead and gives life to them, even so the Son
gives life to whom He will. For the Father judges no one,
but has committed all judgment to the Son, that all should
honor the Son just as they honor the Father. He who
does not honor the Son does not honor the Father who sent
Him. Most assuredly, I say to you, he who hears My
word and believes in Him who sent Me has everlasting
life, and shall not come into judgment,
but has passed from death into life."*
—John 5:1–24

I believe the Word of God is so powerful that it can
transform any and every life. There is power in
God's Word to make that which does not exist to
appear. There is executive power in the words that pro-
ceed from His lips. The psalmist told us, *"He sent His*

Word and healed them" (Ps. 107:20). Do you think the Word has diminished in its power? I tell you, it has not. God's Word can bring things to pass today as it did in the past. The psalmist said, *"Before I was afflicted I went astray, but now I keep Your word"* (Ps. 119:67). And again, *"It is good for me that I have been afflicted, that I may learn Your statutes"* (v. 71). If our afflictions will bring us to the place where we see that we cannot *"live by bread alone, but by every word that proceeds from the mouth of God"* (Matt. 4:4), they will have served a blessed purpose. I want you to realize that there is a life of purity, a life made clean through the Word He has spoken, in which, through faith, you can glorify God with a body that is free from sickness, as well as with a spirit set free from satanic bondage.

Around the pool of Bethesda lay a great multitude of sick folk—blind, lame, paralyzed—waiting for the moving of the water. Did Jesus heal all of them? No, He left many around that pool unhealed. Undoubtedly, many had their eyes on the pool and had no eyes for Jesus. There are many today who always have their confidence in things they can see. If they would only get their eyes on God instead of on natural things, how quickly they would be helped.

The Bread of Healing

The following question arises: Are salvation and healing for all? They are for all who will press right in and claim their portion. Do you remember the case of that Syro-Phoenician woman who wanted the demon cast out of her daughter? Jesus said to her, *"Let the children be filled first, for it is not good to take the children's bread and throw it to the little dogs"* (Mark 7:27). Note that healing and deliverance are here spoken of by the Master as *"the children's bread"*; therefore, if you are a child of God, you can surely press in for your portion.

The Syro-Phoenician woman purposed to get from the Lord what she was after, and she said, *"Yes, Lord, yet even the little dogs under the table eat from the children's crumbs"* (v. 28). Jesus was stirred as He saw this woman's faith, and He told her, *"For this saying go your way; the demon has gone out of your daughter"* (v. 29).

Today many children of God are refusing their blood-purchased portion of health in Christ and are throwing it away. Meanwhile, sinners are pressing through, picking it up from under the table, and finding the cure, not only for their bodies, but also for their spirits and souls. The Syro-Phoenician woman went home and found that the demon had indeed gone out of her daughter. Today there is bread—there is life and health —for every child of God through His powerful Word.

The Word can drive every disease away from your body. Healing is your portion in Christ, who Himself is our bread, our life, our health, our All in All. Though you may be deep in sin, you can come to Him in repentance, and He will forgive and cleanse and heal you. His words are spirit and life to those who will receive them (John 6:63–64). There is a promise in the last verse of Joel that says, *"I will cleanse their blood that I have not cleansed"* (Joel 3:21 KJV). This as much as says that He will provide new life within. The life of Jesus Christ, God's Son, can so purify people's hearts and minds that they become entirely transformed— spirit, soul, and body.

The sick folk were gathered around the pool of Bethesda, and one particular man had been there a long time. His infirmity was of thirty-eight years' standing. Now and again an opportunity to be healed would come as the angel stirred the waters, but he would be sick at heart as he saw another step in and be healed before him. Then one day Jesus was passing that way, and seeing him lying there in that sad condition, He asked, *"Do you want to be made well?"* Jesus said it, and His words are from everlasting to everlasting. These are His words today to you, tried and tested one. You may say, like this poor sick man, "I have missed every opportunity up until now." Never mind that. *"Do you want to be made well?"*

Is It the Lord's Will?

I visited a woman who had been suffering for many years. She was all twisted up with rheumatism and had been in bed two years. I asked her, "What makes you lie here?"

She said, "I've come to the conclusion that I have a thorn in the flesh."

I said, "To what wonderful degree of righteousness have you attained that you must have a thorn in the flesh? Have you had such an abundance of divine revelations that there is a danger of your being exalted above measure?" (See 2 Corinthians 12:7–9.)

She said, "I believe it is the Lord who is causing me to suffer."

I said, "You believe it is the Lord's will for you to suffer, but you are trying to get out of it as quickly as you can. You have medicine bottles all around. Get out of your hiding place, and confess that you are a sinner. If you'll get rid of your self-righteousness, God will do something for you. Drop the idea that you are so holy that God has to afflict you. Sin is the cause of your sickness, not righteousness. Disease is not caused by righteousness, but by sin."

There is healing through the blood of Christ and deliverance for every captive. God never intended His children to live in misery because of some affliction that comes straight from the devil. A perfect atonement was made at Calvary. I believe that Jesus bore my sins, and I am free from them all. I am justified from all things if I dare to believe (Acts 13:39). *"He Himself took our infirmities and bore our sicknesses"* (Matt. 8:17), and if I dare to believe, I can be healed.

See this helpless man at the pool. Jesus asked him, *"Do you want to be made well?"* But there was a difficulty in the way. The man had one eye on the pool and one eye on Jesus. Today, many people are getting crosseyed in the same way. They have one eye on the doctor and one on Jesus. If you will look only to Christ and put both of your eyes on Him, you can be made every bit whole—spirit, soul, and body. It is the promise of the living God that those who *"believe are justified* [made free or innocent] *from all things"* (Acts 13:39). And *"if the Son makes you free, you shall be free indeed"* (John 8:36).

You say, "Oh, if I could only believe!" Jesus understands. He knew that the helpless man had been in that condition for a long time. He is full of compassion. He knows about that kidney trouble; He knows about those corns; He knows about that neuralgia. There is nothing He does not know.

He only wants a chance to show Himself merciful and gracious to you, but He wants to encourage you to believe Him. If you can only believe, you can be saved and healed right now. Dare to believe that Jesus was wounded for your transgressions, was bruised for your iniquities, was chastised that you might have peace, and that by His stripes there is healing for you here and now (Isa. 53:5). You have suffered and failed because you have not believed Him. Cry out to Him even now, *"Lord, I believe; help my unbelief!"* (Mark 9:24).

I was in Long Beach, California, one day. I was with a friend, and we were passing by a hotel. He told me of a doctor there who had a diseased leg. He had been suffering from it for six years and could not get around. We went up to his room and found four other doctors there. I said, "Well, doctor, I see you have plenty going on. I'll come again another day."

I was passing by another time, and the Spirit said, "Go see him." Poor doctor! He surely was in poor shape.

He said, "I have been like this for six years, and nobody can help me."

I said, "You need almighty God."

People are trying to patch up their lives, but they cannot do anything without God. I talked to him for a while about the Lord and then prayed for him.

I cried, "Come out of him in the name of Jesus."

The doctor cried, "It's all gone!"

Oh, if we only knew Jesus! One touch of His might meets the need of every crooked thing. The trouble is getting people to believe Him. The simplicity of this salvation is wonderful. One touch of living faith in Him is all that is required for wholeness to be your portion.

I was in Long Beach about six weeks later, and the sick were coming for prayer. Among those filling up the aisle was the doctor. I said, "What is the trouble?"

He said, "Diabetes, but it will be all right tonight. I know it will be all right."

There is no such thing as the Lord's not meeting your need. There are no *if*s or *may*s; His promises are all *shall*s. *"All things are possible to him who believes"* (Mark 9:23). Oh, the name of Jesus! There is power in that name to meet every human need.

At that meeting there was an old man helping his son to the altar. He said, "He has fits—many every day." Then there was a woman with cancer. Oh, what sin has done!

We read that when God brought forth His people from Egypt, *"there was not one feeble person among their tribes"* (Ps. 105:37 KJV). No disease! All were healed by the power of God! I believe that God wants a people like that today.

I prayed for the woman who had the cancer, and she said, "I know I'm free and that God has delivered me." Then they brought the boy with the fits, and I commanded the evil spirits to leave in the name of Jesus. Then I prayed for the doctor.

At the next night's meeting the house was full. I called out, "Now, doctor, what about the diabetes?"

He said, "It is gone."

Then I said to the old man, "What about your son?"

He said, "He hasn't had any fits since."

We have a God who answers prayer.

Sin and Sickness

Jesus intended this man at the pool to be a testimony forever. When he had both eyes on Jesus, He said to him, "Do the impossible thing. *'Rise, take up your bed and walk.'"* Jesus once called on a man with a withered hand to do the impossible—to stretch forth his hand. The man did the impossible thing. He stretched out his hand,

and it was made completely whole. (See Matthew 12:10–13.)

In the same way, this helpless man began to rise, and he found the power of God moving within him. He wrapped up his bed and began to walk off. It was the Sabbath day, and there were some folks who, because they thought much more of a day than they did of the Lord, began to make a fuss. When the power of God is being manifested, a protest will always come from some hypocrites. Jesus knew all about what the man was going through and met his need again. This time He said to him, *"See, you have been made well. Sin no more, lest a worse thing come upon you."*

There is a close relationship between sin and sickness. How many know that their sicknesses are a direct result of sin? I hope that no one will come to be prayed for who is living in sin. But if you will obey God and repent of your sin and stop it, God will meet you, and neither your sickness nor your sin will remain. *"The prayer of faith will save the sick, and the Lord will raise him up. And if he has committed sins, he will be forgiven"* (James 5:15).

Faith is just the open door through which the Lord comes. Do not say, "I was saved by faith" or "I was healed by faith." Faith does not save and heal. God saves and heals through that open door. You believe, and the power of Christ comes. Salvation and healing are for the glory of God. I am here because God healed me when I was dying; and I have been around the world preaching this full redemption, doing all I can to bring glory to the wonderful name of Jesus, through whom I was healed.

"Sin no more, lest a worse thing come upon you" (John 5:14). The Lord told us in another place about an

evil spirit going out of a man. The house that the evil spirit left got all swept and put in order, but it received no new occupant. The evil spirit, with seven other spirits more wicked than himself, went back to that unoccupied house, and *"the last state of that man* [was] *worse than the first"* (Matt. 12:45).

The Lord does not heal you to go to a baseball game or to a racetrack. He heals you for His glory so that from that moment your life will glorify Him. However, this man remained at a standstill. He did not magnify God. He did not seek to be filled with the Spirit. And his last state became *"worse than the first."*

The Lord wants to so cleanse the motives and desires of our hearts that we will seek one thing only, and that is His glory. I went to a certain place one day, and the Lord said, "This is for My glory." A young man had been sick for a long time. He had been confined to his bed in an utterly hopeless condition. He was fed with a spoon and was never dressed. The weather was damp, so I said to the people in the house, "I wish you would put the young man's clothes by the fire to air." At first they would not take any notice of my request, but because I was persistent, they at last got out his clothes. When they had been aired, I took them into his room.

The Lord said to me, "You will have nothing to do with this," and I just lay prostrate on the floor. The Lord showed me that He was going to shake the place with His glory. The very bed shook. I laid my hands on the young man in the name of Jesus, and the power fell in such a way that I fell with my face to the floor.

In about a quarter of an hour, the young man got up and walked back and forth praising God. He dressed himself and then went out to the room where his father and mother were. He said, "God has healed me." Both the father and mother fell prostrate to the floor as the power of God surged through that room.

There was a woman in that house who had been in an asylum for lunacy, and her condition was so bad that they were about to take her back. But the power of God healed her, too.

The power of God is just the same today as it was in the past. Men need to be taken back to the old paths, to the old-time faith, to believing God's Word and every "Thus says the Lord" in it. The Spirit of the Lord is moving in these days. God is coming forth. If you want to be in the rising tide, you must accept all God has said.

"Do you want to be made well?" (John 5:6). It is Jesus who asks this question. Give Him your answer. He will hear, and He will answer.

Blessing in Australia

The following article is by Sister Winnie Andrews from Melbourne, Australia, in connection with Brother Wigglesworth's ministry there.

A young woman declared: "I was brought to last Sunday's meeting a poor, dying woman, with a disease that was eating into every part of my being. I was full of corruption outside as well as in; but the Lord Jesus Christ came and loosed me and set me free. Since then I have slept better and have eaten more heartily than I have for eight years."

The president of the Methodist Local Preachers' Association testified to having been delivered from nervous trouble.

Mr. Solglush, a prominent businessman, testified to deliverance from an affliction of the feet that he had suffered from since he was two years old—now he is fifty-two. "Since I was prayed for in the name of Jesus, all pain is gone. No one has ever seen me do this (stamping his feet). I have no use for my stick."

A lady said: "While sitting in my seat, listening to the Word, God healed me of liver trouble, gall stones, and sciatica. He also touched my daughter, who was suffering with her feet. Having been operated on twice, she had little hope of being anything but an invalid; but the Lord operated. All pain is gone. Praise the Lord!"

Mr. Lewellyn, a Church of England Reader, testified to having been immediately healed of a stiff knee.

Mr. Barrett testified that Miss Witt of Box Hill, who had been twenty-two years in a wheelchair, rose and walked after Mr. Wigglesworth ministered unto her in the name of Jesus.

Another testified of having been healed the night before of rheumatoid arthritis of four years' standing, and discarded his crutch and walking stick.

Mr. Johnstone of Sperm Vale, who had been deaf for twenty years, and his wife, who had sat in a wheelchair for six years, were immediately healed. The empty chair was wheeled to the railway station, the woman testifying to passersby of the great things God had done for her.

Many were healed through the application of handkerchiefs.

—as reported in *The Pentecostal Evangel*

5

I Am the Lord Who
Heals You

*Is anyone among you sick? Let him call for the
elders of the church, and let them pray over him, anointing
him with oil in the name of the Lord.
And the prayer of faith will save the sick, and
the Lord will raise him up. And if he has
committed sins, he will be forgiven.*
—James 5:14–15

We have in this precious Word a real basis for the truth of healing. In these verses God gives very definite instructions to the sick. If you are sick, your part is to call for the elders of the church; it is their part to anoint and pray for you in faith. Then the whole situation rests with the Lord. When you have been anointed and prayed for, you can rest assured that the Lord will raise you up. It is the Word of God.

I believe that we all can see that the church must not play with this business. If believers turn away from these clear instructions, they are in a place of tremendous danger. Those who refuse to obey do so to their unspeakable loss.

EVER INCREASING FAITH

In connection with this, James told us,

If anyone among you wanders from the truth, and someone turns him back, let him know that he who turns a sinner from the error of his way will save a soul from death and cover a multitude of sins. (James 5:19–20)

Many turn away from the Lord like King Asa, who *"in his disease...did not seek the LORD, but the physicians"* (2 Chron. 16:12). Consequently, *"he died"* (v. 13). I take it that this passage in James means that if one induces another to turn back to the Lord, he will save that person from death, and God will forgive that person of a multitude of sins. This Scripture can also largely apply to salvation. If you turn away from any part of God's truth, the enemy will certainly get an advantage over you.

Does the Lord meet those who look to Him for healing and who obey the instructions set forth in the book of James? Most assuredly. Let me tell you a story to show you how He will undertake for the most extreme case.

A Dying Man Healed

One day I had been visiting the sick and was with a friend of mine, an architect, when I saw a young man from his office coming down the road in a car, holding a telegram in his hand. It contained a very urgent request that we go immediately to pray for a man who was dying. We went off in an auto as fast as possible, and in about an hour and a half reached a large house in the country where the man who was dying resided. There were two staircases in that house. This was extremely convenient, for the doctors could go up and down one, and my friend and I could go up and down the other, and so we had no occasion to meet.

When I arrived, I found that it was a case of this sort: the man's body had been broken, and his bowels had been punctured in two places. The discharge from the bowels had formed abscesses, and blood poisoning had set in. The man's face had turned green. Two doctors were in attendance, but they saw that the case was beyond their power. They had telegraphed London for a great specialist; when we arrived, they were at the railway station awaiting his arrival.

The man was near death and couldn't speak. I said to his wife, "If you desire, we will anoint him and pray."

She said, "That is why I sent for you." I anointed him in the name of Jesus and asked the Lord to raise him up. Apparently, there was no change.

(God often hides what He does. From day to day we find that God is doing wonderful things, and we receive reports of healings that have taken place that we heard nothing about at the time of our meetings. Only last night a woman came into the meeting suffering terribly. Her whole arm was filled with poison, and her blood was so poisoned that it was certain to bring her to her death. We rebuked the thing, and she was here this morning and told us that she was without pain and had slept all night, a thing she had not done for two months. To God be all the praise! You will find He will do this kind of thing all along.)

As soon as we anointed and prayed for this brother, we went down the back staircase, and the three doctors came up the front staircase. As we arrived downstairs, I said to my friend who had come with me, "Friend, let me have hold of your hands." We held each other's hands, and I said to him, "Look into my face and let us agree together, according to Matthew 18:19, that this man will be brought out of this death." We laid the whole matter before God, and said, "Father, we believe."

Then the conflict began. The wife came down to us and said, "The doctors have all their instruments out, and they are about to operate." I cried, "What? Look here. He's your husband, and I tell you this: if those men operate on him, he will die. Go back and tell them you cannot allow it."

She went back to the doctors and said, "Give me ten minutes."

They said, "We can't afford to. Your husband is dying, and it is his only chance."

She said, "I want ten minutes, and you don't touch his body until I have had them."

They went downstairs by one staircase, and we went up by the other. I said to her, "This man is your husband, and he cannot speak for himself. It is now time for you to put your whole trust in God and prove Him wholly true. You can save him from a thousand doctors. You must stand with God and for God in this critical hour."

After that, we came down, and the doctors went up. The wife faced those doctors and said, "You shall not touch this man's body. He is my husband. I am sure that if you operate on him, he will die; but he will live if you don't touch him."

Suddenly, the man in the bed spoke. "God has done it," he said. They rolled back the bedclothes, and the doctors examined him; the abscesses had been cut clear away. The nurse cleaned the place where they had been.

The doctors could see the bowels still open, and they said to the wife, "We know that you have great faith, and we can see that a miracle has taken place. But you must let us unite these broken parts and put in silver tubes. We know that your husband will be all right after that, and it need not interfere with your faith at all."

She said, "God has done the first thing, and He can do the rest. No man shall touch him now." And God healed the whole thing. That man is well and strong today.

Do you ask by what power this was done? I would answer in the words of Peter, *"His name, through faith in His name,...made this man strong"* (Acts 3:16). The anointing was done in the name of the Lord. And it is written, *"The Lord will raise him up."* God provides the double cure, for even if sin has been the cause of the sickness, His Word declares, *"If he has committed sins, he will be forgiven."*

Faith in Jesus and Submission to Others

You ask, "What is faith?" Faith is the principle of the Word of God. The Holy Spirit, who inspired the Word, is called the Spirit of Truth. As we *"receive with meekness the implanted word"* (James 1:21), faith springs up in our hearts—faith in the sacrifice of Calvary; faith in the shed blood of Jesus; faith in the fact that He took our weaknesses upon Himself, bore our sicknesses, carried our pains, and is our Life today.

God has chosen us to help one another. We dare not be independent. He brings us to a place where we submit ourselves to one another. If we refuse to do this, we get away from the Word of God and out of the place of faith. I have been in this place once, and I trust I will never be there again. It happened one time when I went to a meeting. I was very, very sick, and I got worse and worse. I knew the perfect will of God was for me to humble myself and ask the elders to pray for me. I put it off, and the meeting ended. I went home without being anointed and prayed for, and everyone in the house caught the thing I was suffering with.

My boys did not know anything else but to trust the Lord as the family Physician, and my youngest boy, George, cried down from the attic, "Dadda, come."

I cried, "I can't come. The whole thing is from me. I will have to repent and ask the Lord to forgive me." I made up my mind to humble myself before the whole church.

Then I rushed to the attic and laid my hands on my boy in the name of Jesus. I placed my hands on his head, and the pain left and went lower; he cried, "Put your hands lower." This continued until at last the pain went right down to his feet, and as I placed my hands on his feet, he was completely delivered. Some evil power had evidently gotten hold of him, and as I laid my hands on the different parts of his body, it left. (We have to see the difference between anointing the sick and casting out demons.) God will always be gracious when we humble ourselves before Him and come to a place of brokenness of spirit.

One time I was ministering to a sick woman, and she said, "I'm very sick. I become all right for an hour, and then I have another attack." I saw that it was an evil power that was attacking her, and I learned something in that hour that I had never learned before. As I moved my hand down her body in the name of the Lord, that evil power seemed to move just ahead of my hands, and as I moved them down further and further, the evil power went right out of her body and never returned.

Praying for a Paralytic

I was in Le Havre, France, and the power of God was being mightily manifested. A Greek named Felix attended the meeting and became very zealous for God.

He was very eager to get all the Catholics he could to the meeting in order that they could see that God was graciously visiting France. He found a certain bedridden woman who was fixed in a certain position and could not move, and he told her about the Lord's healing at the meetings and said that he would get me to come if she wished. She said, "My husband is a Catholic, and he would never allow anyone who isn't a Catholic to see me."

She asked her husband to allow me to come and told him what Felix had told her about the power of God working in our midst. He said, "I will have no Protestant enter my house."

She said, "You know that the doctors cannot help me, and the priests cannot help. Won't you let this man of God pray for me?" He finally consented, and I went to the house. The simplicity of this woman and her childlike faith were beautiful to see.

I showed her my oil bottle and said, "Here is oil. It is a symbol of the Holy Spirit. When it comes on you, the Holy Spirit will begin to work, and the Lord will raise you up." God did something the moment the oil fell on her. I looked toward the window, and I saw Jesus. (I have seen Him often. There is no painting that is a bit like Him; no artist can ever depict the beauty of my lovely Lord.)

The woman felt the power of God in her body and cried, "I'm free! My hands are free, my shoulders are free, and oh, I see Jesus! I'm free! I'm free!"

The vision vanished, and the woman sat up in bed. Her legs were still bound, and I said to her, "I'll put my hands on your legs, and you will be free entirely." As I put my hands on those legs covered with bedclothes, I looked and saw the Lord again.

She saw Him, too, and cried, "He's there again. I'm free! I'm free!" She rose from her bed and walked around the room praising God, and we were all in tears as we saw His wonderful works.

As we are told in James 5:15, *"the Lord will raise* [them] *up"* when the conditions are met.

"God, Stop This Man!"

When I was a young man, I always loved the fellowship of old men and was always careful to hear what they had to say. I had a friend, an old Baptist minister, who was a wonderful preacher. I spent much of my time with him. One day he came to tell me his wife was dying. I said, "Brother Clark, why don't you believe God? He can raise her up if you will only believe Him." He asked me to come to his house, and I looked for someone to go with me.

I went to a certain rich man who was very zealous for God and spent much money in opening up rescue missions, and I asked him to go with me. He said, "Never you mind me. You go yourself, but I don't take to this kind of business."

Then I thought of a man who could pray by the hour. When he was on his knees, he could go round the world three times and come out at the same place. I asked him to go with me and said to him, "You'll have a real chance this time. Keep at it, and quit when you're through." Some go on after they are through. Brother Nichols, for that was his name, went with me and started praying. He asked the Lord to comfort the husband in his great bereavement and prayed for the orphans and a lot more on this line. I cried, "O God, stop this man!" But there was no stopping him, and he went on praying. There was not a particle of faith in anything he uttered.

When he stopped at last, I said, "Brother Clark, it's now your turn to pray."

He started, "Lord, answer the prayer of my brother and comfort me in this great bereavement and sorrow. Prepare me to face this great trial."

I cried out, "My God, stop this man!" The whole atmosphere was being charged with unbelief.

I had a glass bottle full of oil, and I went up to the woman and poured the whole thing on her in the name of Jesus. Suddenly, Jesus appeared, standing at the foot of the bed. He smiled and then vanished. The woman stood up, perfectly healed, and she is a strong woman today.

Our Wonderful Lord

We have a big God. We have a wonderful Jesus. We have a glorious Comforter. God's canopy is over you and will cover you at all times, preserving you from evil. *"Under his wings shalt thou trust"* (Ps. 91:4 KJV). *"The word of God is living and powerful"* (Heb. 4:12), and in its treasures you will find eternal life. If you dare to trust this wonderful Lord, this Lord of Life, you will find in Him everything you need.

So many are trying drugs, quacks, pills, and plasters. Clear them all out and believe God. It is sufficient to believe God. You will find that if you dare to trust God, He will never fail. *"The prayer of faith will save the sick, and the Lord will raise him up."* Do you trust Him? He is worthy to be trusted.

Delivering a Maniac

One time I was asked to go to Weston-super-Mare, a seaside resort in the western part of England. I learned from a telegram that a man had lost his reason and had

71

become a raving maniac, and some people there wanted me to come and pray for him. I arrived at the place, and the man's wife said to me, "Will you stay with my husband?" I agreed, and in the middle of the night, an evil power laid hold of him. It was awful. I put my hand on his head, and his hair was like toothpicks standing on end. God gave deliverance—a temporary deliverance. At six o'clock the next morning, I felt that it was necessary that I get out of that house for a short time.

The man saw me going and cried out, "If you leave me, there is no hope." But I felt that I had to go.

As I left, I saw a woman with a Salvation Army bonnet on, and I knew that she was going to their 7:00 A.M. prayer meeting. I said to the captain who was in charge of the meeting, when I saw he was about to announce a hymn, "Captain, don't sing. Let's go to prayer." He agreed, and I prayed my heart out. Then I grabbed my hat and rushed out of the hall. They all thought they had had a madman in their prayer meeting that morning.

I saw the man I had spent the night with, rushing down toward the sea without a particle of clothing on, about to drown himself. I cried, "In the name of Jesus, come out of him!" The man fell full length on the ground, and that evil power went out of him never to return. His wife came rushing after him, and the husband was restored to her in a perfect mental condition.

Being Kept by God's Power

There are evil powers, but Jesus is greater than all evil powers. There are tremendous diseases, but Jesus is the Healer. There is no case too hard for Him. The Lion of Judah will break every chain. He came to relieve the oppressed and to set the captive free (Luke 4:18). He came to bring redemption, to make us as perfect as man was before the Fall.

People want to know how to be kept by the power of God. Every position of grace into which you are led—forgiveness, healing, any kind of deliverance—will be contested by the devil. He will contend for your body. When you are saved, the enemy will come around and say, "See, you are not saved." Satan is a liar. If he says you are not saved, it is a sure sign that you are.

You will remember the story of the man whose life was swept clean and put in order. The evil power had been swept out of him. But the man remained in a stationary position. If the Lord heals you, you dare not remain in a stationary position. The evil spirit came back to that man, found his house swept, and took seven others worse than himself and dwelt there. The last state of that man was worse than the first. (See Matthew 12:43–45.) Be sure to get filled with God. Get an Occupier. Be filled with the Spirit.

God has a million ways of undertaking for those who go to Him for help. He has deliverance for *every* captive. He loves you so much that He even says, *"Before they call, I will answer"* (Isa. 65:24). Don't turn Him away.

≈⊹═⊷⊹≈

A Letter of Testimony from San Diego

I slipped and fell on Broadway, San Diego, in February 1921, and as was afterward discovered, fractured the coccyx (the base of the spine), and so severely wrenched the hips and pelvic bones that I became a great sufferer. As the broken bone was not discovered until about two months after the accident, the constant pain and irritation caused a general inflammation of the nervous system, and the long delay in getting the bone set made it impossible to heal, so that my condition grew steadily worse. I was taken to the hospital, and the bone was removed about a month after it had been set. Though the wound healed rapidly, the nervous inflammation remained, and so for many months longer I was in constant pain and unable to get around without assistance.

I was taken to the first service held by Mr. Wigglesworth on the 2nd of October, 1922. At the close of the service, all those who were sick and in pain and had come for healing were requested to rise if possible. My husband assisted me to my feet, and as we were prayed for by the speaker (Mr. Wigglesworth), I was instantly healed. How I do not know. I only know the Great Physician touched my body, and I was made whole and freed from pain.

After I got home, I showed how I could sit down and rise with my hands above my head, when before it had taken both hands to push up my feeble body, and I had to have straps on my bed to pull myself up with. No more use for them now! I lay down and turned over for the first time without pain. I shall never cease to praise God for the healing of my body through the precious blood of Jesus and in His name. I walked to the streetcar alone the next day and attended the next service and have been "on the go" ever since.

—written by *Mrs. Sanders*
San Diego, California

6

He Himself Took
Our Infirmities

*When He had come down from the mountain, great
multitudes followed Him. And behold, a leper came and
worshiped Him, saying, "Lord, if You are willing, You can
make me clean." Then Jesus put out His hand and touched
him, saying, "I am willing; be cleansed." Immediately his
leprosy was cleansed. And Jesus said to him, "See that you
tell no one; but go your way, show yourself to the priest, and
offer the gift that Moses commanded, as a testimony to them."
Now when Jesus had entered Capernaum, a centurion came
to Him, pleading with Him, saying, "Lord, my servant is
lying at home paralyzed, dreadfully tormented." And Jesus
said to him, "I will come and heal him." The centurion
answered and said, "Lord, I am not worthy that You should
come under my roof. But only speak a word, and my servant
will be healed. "For I also am a man under authority, having
soldiers under me. And I say to this one, 'Go,' and he goes;
and to another, 'Come,' and he comes; and to my servant,
'Do this,' and he does it." When Jesus heard it, He
marveled, and said to those who followed, "Assuredly, I say
to you, I have not found such great faith, not even in Israel!
And I say to you that many will come from east and west,
and sit down with Abraham, Isaac, and Jacob in the*

kingdom of heaven. "But the sons of the kingdom will be
cast out into outer darkness. There will be weeping and
gnashing of teeth." Then Jesus said to the centurion,
"Go your way; and as you have believed, so let it be done
for you." And his servant was healed that same hour.
Now when Jesus had come into Peter's house, He saw
his wife's mother lying sick with a fever. So He touched
her hand, and the fever left her. And she arose and served
them. And He cast out the spirits with a word, and
healed all who were sick, that it might be fulfilled
which was spoken by Isaiah the prophet, saying:
"He Himself took our infirmities
and bore our sicknesses."
—Matthew 8:16–17

H ere we have a wonderful word. All of the Word is wonderful. This blessed Book brings such life, health, peace, and abundance that we should never be poor anymore. This Book is my heavenly bank. I find everything I want in it. I desire to show you how rich you may be, so that in everything you can be enriched in Christ Jesus (1 Cor. 1:5). For you He has *"abundance of grace and...the gift of righteousness"* (Rom. 5:17), and through His abundant grace *"all things are possible"* (Matt. 19:26). I want to show you that you can be a living branch of the living Vine, Christ Jesus, and that it is your privilege to be, right here in this world, what He is. John told us, *"As He is, so are we in this world"* (1 John 4:17). Not that we are anything in ourselves, but Christ within us is our All in All.

The Lord Jesus always wants to show forth His grace and love in order to draw us to Himself. God is willing to do things, to manifest His Word, and to let us know a measure of the mind of our God in this day and hour.

He Himself Took Our Infirmities

A Leper Is Miraculously Cleansed

Today there are many needy, many afflicted ones, but I do not think anyone present is half as bad as the first case that we read of in the eighth chapter of Matthew:

When He had come down from the mountain, great multitudes followed Him. And behold, a leper came and worshiped Him, saying, "Lord, if You are willing, You can make me clean." Then Jesus put out His hand and touched him, saying, "I am willing; be cleansed." Immediately his leprosy was cleansed. And Jesus said to him, "See that you tell no one; but go your way, show yourself to the priest, and offer the gift that Moses commanded, as a testimony to them." (Matt. 8:1–4)

This man was a leper. You may be suffering from tuberculosis, cancer, or other things, but God will show forth His perfect cleansing, His perfect healing, if you have a living faith in Christ. He is a wonderful Jesus.

This leper must have been told about Jesus. How much is missed because people are not constantly telling what Jesus will do in our day. Probably someone had come to that leper and said, "Jesus can heal you." So he was filled with expectation as he saw the Lord coming down the mountainside. Lepers were not allowed to come within reach of other people; they were shut out as unclean. Ordinarily, it would have been very difficult for him to get near because of the crowd that surrounded Jesus. But as Jesus came down from the mountain, He met this poor leper.

Oh, leprosy is a terrible disease! There was no help for him, humanly speaking, but nothing is too hard for Jesus. The man cried, *"Lord, if You are willing, You can make me clean"* (Matt. 8:2). Was Jesus willing? You will never find Jesus missing an opportunity to do good. You will find that He is always more willing to work than we are to give Him an opportunity to work. The trouble is that we do not come to Him; we do not ask Him for what He is more than willing to give.

"Then Jesus put out His hand and touched him, saying, 'I am willing; be cleansed.' Immediately his leprosy was cleansed" (v. 3). I like that. If you are definite with Him, you will never go away disappointed. The divine life will flow into you, and instantaneously you will be delivered. This Jesus is just the same today, and He says to you, *"I am willing; be cleansed."* He has an overflowing cup for you, a fullness of life. He will meet you in your absolute helplessness. All things are possible if you will only believe (Mark 9:23). God has a real plan. It is very simple: just come to Jesus. You will find Him just the same as He was in days of old (Heb. 13:8).

Jesus Heals by Saying a Word

The next case we have in Matthew 8 is that of the centurion coming and pleading with Jesus on behalf of his servant, who was paralyzed and was dreadfully tormented.

> *Now when Jesus had entered Capernaum, a centurion came to Him, pleading with Him, saying, "Lord, my servant is lying at home paralyzed, dreadfully tormented." And Jesus said to him, "I will come and heal him." The centurion answered and said, "Lord, I am not worthy that You should come under my roof. But only speak a word, and my servant will be healed. For I also am a man*

under authority, having soldiers under me. And I say to this one, 'Go,' and he goes; and to another, 'Come,' and he comes; and to my servant, 'Do this,' and he does it." When Jesus heard it, He marveled, and said to those who followed, "Assuredly, I say to you, I have not found such great faith, not even in Israel! And I say to you that many will come from east and west, and sit down with Abraham, Isaac, and Jacob in the kingdom of heaven. But the sons of the kingdom will be cast out into outer darkness. There will be weeping and gnashing of teeth." Then Jesus said to the centurion, "Go your way; and as you have believed, so let it be done for you." And his servant was healed that same hour. (Matt. 8:5–13)

This man was so in earnest that he came seeking Jesus. Notice that there is one thing certain: there is no such thing as seeking without finding. *"He who seeks finds"* (Matt. 7:8). Listen to the gracious words of Jesus: *"I will come and heal him"* (Matt. 8:7).

Jesus Loves to Heal

In most places where I go, there are many people for whom I cannot pray. In some places there are two or three hundred people who would like me to visit them, but I am not able to do so. Yet I am glad that the Lord Jesus is always willing to come and heal. He longs to help the sick ones. He loves to heal them of their afflictions. The Lord is healing many people today by means of handkerchiefs, even as He did in the days of Paul. (See Acts 19:11–12.)

A woman came to me in the city of Liverpool and said, "I would like you to help me by joining me in prayer. My husband is a drunkard, and every night he comes into the home under the influence of drink. Will you join me in prayer for him?"

I asked the woman, "Do you have a handkerchief?" She took out a handkerchief, and I prayed over it and told her to lay it on the pillow of the drunken man. He came home that night and laid his head on the pillow in which this handkerchief had been tucked. He laid his head on more than the pillow that night, because he laid his head on the promise of God. In Mark 11:24, we read, *"Whatever things you ask when you pray, believe that you receive them, and you will have them."*

The next morning the man got up and, going into the first saloon that he had to pass on his way to work, ordered some beer. He tasted it and said to the bartender, "You put some poison in this beer."

He could not drink it, and he went on to the next saloon and ordered some more beer. He tasted it and said to the man behind the counter, "You put some poison in this beer. I believe you folks have plotted to poison me." The bartender was indignant at being charged with this crime. The man said, "I will go somewhere else."

He went to another tavern, and the same thing happened as in the two previous places. He made such a fuss that he was thrown out.

After he left work that evening, he went to another tavern to get some beer, and again he thought the bartender was trying to poison him. Once again he made such a disturbance that he was thrown out of that saloon. He went to his home and told his wife what had happened and said, "It seems as though all the fellows have agreed to poison me."

His wife said to him, "Can't you see the hand of the Lord in this and that He is making you dislike the stuff that has been your ruin?" This word brought conviction to the man's heart, and he came to the meeting and got saved. The Lord still has power to set the captives free.

When I was in Australia, a lady came to me who was much troubled about her son, who was very lazy. I prayed over a handkerchief, which was placed in the boy's pillow. He slept that night on the handkerchief. The next morning, he got up, went out, secured a job, and went to work. Oh, praise the Lord, you can't shut out God; but if you will only believe, He will shut out the devil.

Jesus was willing to go and heal the sick servant, but the centurion said, *"Lord, I am not worthy that You should come under my roof. But only speak a word, and my servant will be healed"* (Matt. 8:8).

Jesus was delighted with this expression and *"said to the centurion, 'Go your way; and as you have believed, so let it be done for you.' And his servant was healed that same hour"* (v. 13).

Let me tell you about something else that happened when I was in Australia. A man came up to me leaning on a big stick, and he said, "I would like you to help me. It will take you half an hour to pray for me."

I said, "Believe God, and in one moment you will be whole." His faith was quickened to receive an immediate healing, and He went away glorifying God for a miraculous healing.

The Word of the Lord is sufficient today. If you will dare to believe God's Word, you will see a performance of His Word that will be truly wonderful. With the centurion we have an audacity of faith, a faith that did not limit God. Failures come when we limit the Holy One of Israel. I want to encourage you to a living faith to believe God's Word.

EVER INCREASING FAITH

Peter's Mother-in-Law Healed

*Now when Jesus had come into Peter's house, He
saw his wife's mother lying sick with a fever. So He
touched her hand, and the fever left her. And she
arose and served them.* (Matt. 8:14–15)

The next healing we read of is the healing of Peter's
wife's mother, who was sick with a fever. Luke tells us
that Jesus *"rebuked the fever"* (Luke 4:39). The fever
could hear. The moment it could hear, it went. Jesus had
a new method.

Today, there are a lot of folks who try to sweat out a
fever, but you can't sweat the devil out. He can stand all
the heat that you can apply to him. However, *"if you can
believe"* (Mark 9:23), deliverance is as sure and certain
for you as it was for Peter's mother-in-law.

Facing a Demon-Possessed Woman

I received a telegram once urging me to visit a case
about two hundred miles from my home. As I went to
this place, I met the father and mother and found them
brokenhearted. They led me up a staircase to a room,
and I saw a young woman on the floor. Five men were
holding her down. She was a frail young woman, but the
power in her was greater than the strength of all those
young men. As I went into the room, the evil powers
looked out of her eyes, and they used her lips, saying,
"We are many; you can't cast us out."

I said, "Jesus can."

Jesus is equal to every occasion. He is waiting for an
opportunity to bless. He is ready for every opportunity to
deliver souls. When we receive Jesus, the following verse

is true of us: *"Greater is he that is in* [us], *than he that is in the world"* (1 John 4:4 KJV). He is greater than all the powers of darkness. No man can meet the devil in his own strength, but any man filled with the knowledge of Jesus, filled with His presence, filled with His power, is more than a match for the powers of darkness. God has called us to be *"more than conquerors through Him who loved us"* (Rom. 8:37).

The living Word is able to destroy satanic forces. There is power in the name of Jesus. I wish that every window on the street had the name of Jesus written on it in large letters.

Through faith in His name, deliverance was brought to this poor bound soul, and thirty-seven demons came out of her, giving their names as they came forth. The dear woman was completely delivered, and the family was able to give her back her child. That night there was heaven in that home, and the father, mother, son, and his wife were all united in glorifying Christ for His infinite grace. The next morning we had a gracious time in the breaking of bread.

All things are wonderful with our wonderful Jesus. If you would dare rest your all upon Him, things would take place, and He would change the whole situation. In a moment, through the name of Jesus, a new order of things can be brought in.

In the world, new diseases are always surfacing, and the doctors cannot identify them. A doctor said to me, "The science of medicine is in its infancy, and we doctors really have no confidence in our medicine. We are always experimenting." But the man of God does not experiment. He knows, or ought to know, redemption in its fullness. He knows, or ought to know, the mightiness of the Lord Jesus Christ. He is not, or should not, be moved by outward observation but should get a divine revelation of the mightiness of the name of Jesus and the power of His blood. If we exercise our faith in the Lord Jesus Christ, He will come forth and get glory over all the powers of darkness.

Christ Bore Our Sicknesses and Sin

When evening had come, they brought to Him many who were demon-possessed. And He cast out the spirits with a word, and healed all who were sick, that it might be fulfilled which was spoken by Isaiah the prophet, saying: "He Himself took our infirmities and bore our sicknesses."

(Matt. 8:16–17)

The work is done if you only believe it. It is done. *"He Himself took our infirmities and bore our sicknesses."* If only you can see the Lamb of God going to Calvary! He took our flesh so that He could take upon Himself the full burden of all our sin and all the consequences of sin. There on the cross of Calvary, God laid upon Him the iniquities of us all (Isa. 53:6). There on the cross, the results of sin were also dealt with.

Inasmuch then as the children have partaken of flesh and blood, He Himself likewise shared in the same, that through death He might destroy him who had the power of death, that is, the devil, and release those who through fear of death were all their lifetime subject to bondage. (Heb. 2:14–15)

Through Jesus' death, there is deliverance for you today.

❧ ✢══✢ ☙

Husband Healed of Double Rupture and Other Ills

One year ago my husband was instantly healed of a double rupture of three years' standing, dropsy (two years), a weak heart, and tobacco chewing (forty-seven years). Praise the Lord, it was all taken away when the shock from heaven's battery went through him.

Nine weeks ago today we went to Portland, Oregon, to hear Brother Smith Wigglesworth, and my husband was healed instantly of high blood pressure and varicose veins that had broken in his ankles and for a year had to be dressed twice a day. No doctor could help him, but, praise God, Jesus was the doctor and healed him.

—written by *Mrs. Frank Nephews*
Newberg, Oregon

7

Our Risen Christ

Now as they spoke to the people, the priests, the captain of the temple, and the Sadducees came upon them, being greatly disturbed that they taught the people and preached in Jesus the resurrection from the dead. And they laid hands on them, and put them in custody until the next day, for it was already evening. However, many of those who heard the word believed; and the number of the men came to be about five thousand. And it came to pass, on the next day, that their rulers, elders, and scribes, as well as Annas the high priest, Caiaphas, John, and Alexander, and as many as were of the family of the high priest, were gathered together at Jerusalem. And when they had set them in the midst, they asked, "By what power or by what name have you done this?" Then Peter, filled with the Holy Spirit, said to them, "Rulers of the people and elders of Israel: If we this day are judged for a good deed done to a helpless man, by what means he has been made well, let it be known to you all, and to all the people of Israel, that by the name of Jesus Christ of Nazareth, whom you crucified, whom God raised from the dead, by Him this man stands here before you whole. This is the 'stone which was rejected by you builders, which has become the chief cornerstone.' Nor is there salvation in any other, for there is no other name under heaven given among men by which we must be saved."

EVER INCREASING FAITH

Now when they saw the boldness of Peter and John, and perceived that they were uneducated and untrained men, they marveled. And they realized that they had been with Jesus. And seeing the man who had been healed standing with them, they could say nothing against it. But when they had commanded them to go aside out of the council, they conferred among themselves, saying, "What shall we do to these men? For, indeed, that a notable miracle has been done through them is evident to all who dwell in Jerusalem, and we cannot deny it. But so that it spreads no further among the people, let us severely threaten them, that from now on they speak to no man in this name." And they called them and commanded them not to speak at all nor teach in the name of Jesus. But Peter and John answered and said to them, "Whether it is right in the sight of God to listen to you more than to God, you judge. For we cannot but speak the things which we have seen and heard." So when they had further threatened them, they let them go, finding no way of punishing them, because of the people, since they all glorified God for what had been done. For the man was over forty years old on whom this miracle of healing had been performed. And being let go, they went to their own companions and reported all that the chief priests and elders had said to them. So when they heard that, they raised their voice to God with one accord and said: "Lord, You are God, who made heaven and earth and the sea, and all that is in them, who by the mouth of Your servant David have said: 'Why did the nations rage, and the people plot vain things? The kings of the earth took their stand, and the rulers were gathered together against the LORD and against His Christ.' For truly against Your holy Servant Jesus, whom You anointed, both Herod and Pontius Pilate, with the Gentiles and the people of Israel, were gathered together to do whatever Your hand and Your purpose determined before to be done. Now, Lord, look on their threats, and grant to

Our Risen Christ

Your servants that with all boldness they may speak Your word, by stretching out Your hand to heal, and that signs and wonders may be done through the name of Your holy Servant Jesus." And when they had prayed, the place where they were assembled together was shaken; and they were all filled with the Holy Spirit, and they spoke the word of God with boldness. Now the multitude of those who believed were of one heart and one soul; neither did anyone say that any of the things he possessed was his own, but they had all things in common. And with great power the apostles gave witness to the resurrection of the Lord Jesus. And great grace was upon them all. Nor was there anyone among them who lacked; for all who were possessors of lands or houses sold them, and brought the proceeds of the things that were sold, and laid them at the apostles' feet; and they distributed to each as anyone had need. And Joses, who was also named Barnabas by the apostles (which is translated Son of Encouragement), a Levite of the country of Cyprus, having land, sold it, and brought the money and laid it at the apostles' feet.
—Acts 4

We praise God that our glorious Jesus is the risen Christ. Those of us who have tasted the power of the indwelling Spirit know something about how the hearts of those two disciples burned as they walked to Emmaus with the risen Lord as their companion. (See Luke 24:13–31.)

Note the words of Acts 4:31: *"And when they had prayed, the place where they were assembled together was shaken."* There are many churches where they never pray the kind of prayer that you read of here. A church that does not know how to pray and to shout will never be shaken. If you live or worship in a place like that, you might as well write over the threshold: *"Ich-abod...The glory has departed from Israel!"* (1 Sam. 4:21). It is only when men have learned the secret of prayer, power, and praise that God comes forth. Some people say, "Well, I praise God inwardly," but if there is an abundance of praise in your heart, your mouth cannot help speaking it.

What Is Inside Will Come Out

A man who had a large business in London was a great churchgoer. The church he attended was beautifully decorated, and his pew was delightfully cushioned— just enough to make it easy to sleep through the sermons. He was a prosperous man in business, but he had no peace in his heart. There was a boy at his business who always looked happy. He was always jumping and whistling. One day he said to this boy, "I want to see you in my office."

When the boy came to his office, the man asked him, "How is it that you can always whistle and be happy?"

"I cannot help it," answered the boy.

"Where did you get this happiness?" asked the gentleman.

"I got it at the Pentecostal mission."

"Where is that?" The boy told him, and the man began attending. The Lord reached his heart, and in a short while, he was entirely changed. One day, shortly after this, he found that instead of being distracted by his business as he formerly had been, he was actually whistling and jumping. His disposition and his whole life had been changed.

The shout cannot come out unless it is within. The inner working of the power of God must come first. It is

He who changes the heart and transforms the life. Before there is any real outward evidence, there must be the inflow of divine life.

Sometimes I say to people, "You weren't at the meeting the other night."

They reply, "Oh, yes, I was there in spirit."

I say to them, "Well, next time come with your body also. We don't want a lot of spirits here and no bodies. We want you to come and get filled with God."

When all the people come and pray and praise as did these early disciples, there will be something happening. People who come will catch fire, and they will want to come again; but they will have no use for a place where everything has become formal, dry, and dead.

The power of Pentecost came to loose men. God wants us to be free. Men and women are tired of imitations; they want reality; they want to see people who have the living Christ within, who are filled with Holy Spirit power.

God Is Always on Time

I received several letters and telegrams about a certain case, but when I arrived, I was told I was too late. I said, "That cannot be. God has never sent me anywhere too late." God showed me that something different would happen than anything I had ever seen before. The people I went to were all strangers.

I was introduced to a young man who lay helpless, and for whom there was no hope. The doctor had been to see him that morning and had declared that he would not live through the day. He lay with his face to the wall, and when I spoke to him, he whispered, "I cannot turn over." His mother said that they had had to lift him out of bed on sheets for weeks, and that he was so frail and helpless that he had to stay in one position.

The young man said, "My heart is very weak." I assured him, " *'God is the strength of* [your] *heart and* [your] *portion forever'* (Ps. 73:26). If you will believe God, it will be so today."

Our Christ is risen. He is a living Christ who lives within us. We must not have this truth merely as a theory. Christ must be risen in us by the power of the Spirit. The power that raised Him from the dead must animate us, and as this glorious resurrection power surges through our beings, we will be freed from all our weaknesses. We will *"be strong in the Lord and in the power of His might"* (Eph. 6:10). There is a resurrection power that God wants you to have and to have today. Why not receive your portion here and now?

I said to these people, "I believe your son will rise today." They only laughed. People do not expect to see signs and wonders today as the disciples saw them of old. Has God changed, or has our faith diminished so that we are not expecting the greater works that Jesus promised? We must not sing in any minor key. Our message must rise to concert pitch, and there must be nothing left out that is in the Book.

It was wintertime, and I said to the parents, "Will you get the boy's suit and bring it here?" They would not listen to the request, because they were expecting the boy to die. But I had gone to that place believing God. We read about Abraham:

(As it is written, "I have made you a father of many nations") in the presence of Him whom he believed; God…gives life to the dead and calls those things which do not exist as though they did. (Rom. 4:17)

May God help us to understand this. It is time people knew how to shout in faith as they contemplate the eternal power of our God, to whom it is nothing to *"give life to your mortal bodies"* (Rom. 8:11) and raise the dead. I come across some who would be giants in the power of God, but they have no shout of faith. Everywhere, I find people who become discouraged even when they are praying simply because they are just breathing sentences without uttering speech. You cannot win the victory that way. You must learn to take the victory and shout in the face of the devil, "It is done!"

There is no man who can doubt if he learns to shout. When we know how to shout properly, things will be different, and tremendous things will happen. In Acts 4:24 we read, *"They raised their voice to God with one accord."* It surely must have been a loud prayer. We must know that God means for us to have life. If there is anything in the world that has life in it, it is this Pentecostal revival we are in. I believe in the baptism of the Holy Spirit with the speaking in tongues, and I believe that every man who is baptized in the Holy Spirit will *"speak with other tongues, as the Spirit* [gives him] *utterance"* (Acts 2:4). I believe in the Holy Spirit. And if you are filled with the Spirit, you will be superabounding in life, and living waters will flow from you.

At last I persuaded the parents to bring the boy's clothes and lay them on the bed. From the human viewpoint, the young man lay dying. I spoke to the afflicted lad, "God has revealed to me that as I lay my hands on you, the place will be filled with the Holy Spirit, the bed will be shaken, you will be shaken and thrown out of bed by the power of the Holy Spirit, and you will dress yourself and be strong." I said this to him in faith. I laid hands on him in the name of Jesus, and instantly the power of

God fell and filled the place. I felt helpless and fell flat on the floor. I knew nothing except that a short while after the place was shaken.

Then I heard the young man walking over me and saying, "For Your glory, Lord! For Your glory, Lord!"

He dressed himself and cried, "God has healed me." The father fell, the mother fell, and another who was present also fell. God manifested His power that day in saving the whole household and healing the young man. It is the power of the risen Christ we need. Today, that young man is preaching the Gospel.

God Is at Work

For years we have been longing for God to come forth, and, praise Him, He is coming forth. The tide is rising everywhere. I was in Switzerland not long ago, preaching in many places where the Pentecostal message had not been heard. Today, there are nine new Pentecostal assemblies in different places going on blessedly for God. All over the world it is the same; this great Pentecostal work is in motion. You can hardly go to a place now where God is not pouring out His Spirit upon hungry hearts. God has promised to pour out His Spirit upon all flesh, and His promises never fail. Our Christ is risen. His salvation was not a thing done in a corner. Truly He was a man of glory who went to Calvary for us in order that He might free us from all that would mar and hinder, that He might transform us by His grace and bring us out from under the power of the enemy into the glorious power of God. One touch of our risen Christ will raise the dead. Hallelujah!

Oh, this wonderful Jesus of ours comes and indwells us! He comes to abide. It is He who baptizes us with the

Holy Spirit and makes everything different. We are to be a *"kind of firstfruits"* (James 1:18) unto God and are to be like Christ who is the First Fruit. We are to walk in His footsteps and live in His power. What a salvation this is, having this risen Christ in us. I feel that everything else must go to nothingness, helplessness, and ruin. Even the best thought of holiness must be on the decrease in order that Christ may increase. All things are under the power of the Spirit.

God Is with You

Dare you take your inheritance from God? Dare you believe God? Dare you stand on the record of His Word? What is the record? If you will believe, you will see the glory of God (John 11:40). You will be sifted as wheat. You will be tested as though some strange thing tried you. (See 1 Peter 4:12.) You will be put in places where you will have to put your whole trust in God. There is no such thing as anyone being tested beyond what God will allow. There is no temptation that will come, but God will be with you right in the temptation to deliver you (1 Cor. 10:13), and when you have been tried, He will bring you forth as gold (Job 23:10). Every trial is to bring you to a greater position in God. The trial that tries your faith will take you on to the place where you will know that the faith of God will be forthcoming in the next test. No man is able to win any victory except through the power of the risen Christ within him. You will never be able to say, "I did this or that." You will desire to give God the glory for everything.

If you are sure of your ground, if you are counting on the presence of the living Christ within, you can laugh when you see things getting worse. God wants you to be settled and grounded in Christ, and it is only as you are filled with the Holy Spirit that you become steadfast and unmoveable in Him.

The Lord Jesus said, *"I have a baptism to be baptized with, and how distressed I am till it is accomplished!"* (Luke 12:50). Assuredly, He was distressed all along the way: in Gethsemane, in the judgment hall, and, after that, on the cross, where He, *"through the eternal Spirit offered Himself without spot to God"* (Heb. 9:14). God will take us right on in like manner, and the Holy Spirit will lead every step of the way. God led Him right through to the empty tomb, to the glory of the Ascension, to a place on the throne. The Son of God will never be satisfied until He has us with Himself, sharing His glory and sharing His throne.

8

Righteousness

You have loved righteousness
and hated lawlessness; therefore God, Your God
has anointed You with the oil of gladness
more than Your companions.
—Hebrews 1:9

As we are indwelt by the Holy Spirit, God purposes that, like our Lord, we should love righteousness and hate lawlessness. I see that there is a place for us in Christ Jesus where we are no longer under condemnation but where the heavens are always open to us. I see that God has a realm of divine life opening up to us where there are boundless possibilities, where there is limitless power, where there are untold resources, and where we have victory over all the power of the devil. I believe that, as we are filled with the desire to press on into this life of true holiness, desiring only the glory of God, nothing can hinder our true advancement.

Precious Faith

Peter began his second letter with these words:

97

Ever Increasing Faith

Simon Peter, a bondservant and apostle of Jesus Christ, to those who have obtained like precious faith with us by the righteousness of our God and Savior Jesus Christ. (2 Pet. 1:1)

Through faith, we realize that we have a blessed and glorious union with our risen Lord. When He was on earth, Jesus told us, *"I am in the Father and the Father in Me"* (John 14:11). *"The Father who dwells in Me does the works"* (v. 10). And He prayed to His Father, not only for His disciples, but for those who would believe on Him through their testimonies: *"That they all may be one, as You, Father, are in Me, and I in You; that they also may be one in Us, that the world may believe that You sent me"* (John 17:21). What an inheritance is ours when the very nature, the very righteousness, the very power of the Father and the Son are made real in us. This is God's purpose, and as by faith, we take hold of the purpose, we will always be conscious that *"He who is in* [us] *is greater than he who is in the world"* (1 John 4:4). The purpose of all Scripture is to move us to this wonderful and blessed elevation of faith where our constant experience is the manifestation of God's life and power through us.

Peter goes on writing to those who have obtained *"like precious faith,"* saying, *"Grace and peace be multiplied to you in the knowledge of God and of Jesus our Lord"* (2 Pet. 1:2). We can have the multiplication of this grace and peace only as we live in the realm of faith. Abraham attained to the place where he became a *"friend of God"* because he *"believed God"* (James 2:23). He *"believed God, and it was accounted to him for righteousness"* (v. 23). Righteousness was credited to him on no other ground than that he *"believed God."* Can this be true of anybody else? Yes, every person in the whole world who is saved by faith is blessed along with faithful Abraham. The promise that came to him because he believed God was that in him all the families of the earth would be blessed (Gen. 18:18). When we believe God, there is no telling where the blessings of our faith will end.

Some are anxious because, when they are prayed for, the thing that they are expecting does not happen that same night. They say they believe, but you can see that they are really in turmoil from their unbelief. Abraham believed God. You can hear him saying to Sarah, "Sarah, there is no life in you, and there is nothing in me; but God has promised us a son, and I believe God." That kind of faith is a joy to our Father in heaven.

Eyes of Faith

One day I was having a meeting in Bury, in Lancashire, England. A young woman from a place called Ramsbottom came to be healed of a goiter. Before she came she said, "I am going to be healed of this goiter, Mother." After one meeting, she came forward and was prayed for. The next meeting she got up and testified that she had been wonderfully healed. She said, "I will be so happy to go and tell Mother about my healing."

She went to her home and testified how wonderfully she had been healed. The next year when we were having the convention, she came again. From a human perspective, it looked as though the goiter was just as big as ever, but that young woman was believing God. Soon she was on her feet giving her testimony, saying, "I was here last year, and the Lord wonderfully healed me. I want to tell you that this has been the best year of my life." She seemed to be greatly blessed in that meeting, and she went home to testify more strongly than ever that the Lord had healed her.

She believed God. The third year, she was at the meeting again, and some people who looked at her said, "Look how big that goiter has become!" But when the time came for testimonies, she was on her feet and testified, "Two years ago, the Lord gloriously healed me of a goiter. Oh, I had a most wonderful healing. It is grand to be healed by the power of God."

That day someone questioned her and said, "People will think there is something the matter with you. Why don't you look in the mirror? You will see your goiter is bigger than ever." The young woman went to the Lord about it and said, "Lord, You so wonderfully healed me two years ago. Won't You show all the people that You healed me?" She went to sleep peacefully that night still believing God. When she came down the next day, there was not a trace or a mark of that goiter.

The Mirror of Faith

God's Word is from everlasting to everlasting. His Word cannot fail. God's Word is true, and when we rest in its truth, what mighty results we can get. Faith never looks in the mirror. The mirror of faith is the perfect law of liberty:

> But he who looks into the perfect law of liberty and continues in it, and is not a forgetful hearer but a doer of the work, this one will be blessed in what he does.   (James 1:25)

To the man who looks into this perfect law of God, all darkness is removed. He sees his completeness in Christ.

Righteousness

There is no darkness in faith. Darkness is only in nature. Darkness exists when the natural replaces the divine.

Grace and peace are multiplied to us through a knowledge of God and of Jesus Christ. As we really know our God, and Jesus Christ, whom He has sent, we will have peace multiplied to us even in the multiplied fires of ten thousand Nebuchadnezzars. (See Daniel 3:10–30.) Our peace will be multiplied to us even though we are put into a den of lions, and we will live with joy in the middle of the whole thing.

What was the difference between Daniel and the king that night when Daniel was put into the den of lions? Daniel's faith was certain, but the king's faith was experimental. The king came around the next morning and cried, *"Daniel, servant of the living God, has your God, whom you serve continually, been able to deliver you from the lions?"* (Dan. 6:20). Daniel answered, *"My God sent His angel and shut the lions' mouths"* (v. 22). The thing was done. It was done when Daniel prayed with his windows open toward heaven.

All our victories are won before we go into the fight. They are won as we pray. Prayer links us to our lovely God, our peaceful God, our abounding God, our multiplying God. Oh, I love Him. He is so wonderful!

Holiness Opens the Door

You will note as you read 2 Peter 1:1–2 that this grace and peace are multiplied through the knowledge of God, but that first our faith comes through the righteousness of God. Note that righteousness comes first and knowledge afterwards. It cannot be otherwise. If you expect any revelation of God apart from holiness, you will have only a mixture. Holiness opens the door to all the treasures of God. He must first bring us to the place where we, like our Lord, love righteousness and hate lawlessness (Heb. 1:9), before He opens up to us these good treasures. When we *"regard iniquity in* [our hearts], *the Lord will not hear"* us (Ps. 66:18); and it is only as we are made righteous, pure, and holy through the precious blood of God's Son that we can enter into this life of holiness and righteousness in the Son. It is the righteousness of our Lord Himself made real in us as our faith remains in Him.

After I was baptized with the Holy Spirit, the Lord gave me a blessed revelation. I saw Adam and Eve turned out of the Garden for their disobedience. They were unable to partake of the Tree of Life, for the cherubim with flaming sword kept them away from this tree. When I was baptized, I saw that I had begun to eat of this Tree of Life, and I saw that the flaming sword surrounded it. It was there to keep the devil away. Oh, what privileges are ours when we are born of God! How marvelously He keeps us so that the wicked one cannot touch us. I see a place in God where the enemy does not dare to come. We are *"hidden with Christ in God"* (Col. 3:3). He invites us all to come and share this wonderful hidden place. We dwell *"in the secret place of the Most High"* and *"abide under the shadow of the Almighty"* (Ps. 91:1). God has this place for you in this blessed realm of grace.

Peter went on to say, *"As His divine power has given to us all things that pertain to life and godliness, through the knowledge of Him who called us by glory and virtue"* (2 Pet. 1:3). God is calling us to this realm of glory and virtue where, as we feed on His *"exceedingly great and precious promises,"* we are made *"partakers of the divine nature"* (v. 4).

Righteousness

Dare to Believe God

"Faith is the substance of things hoped for" (Heb. 11:1) right here in this life. It is here that God wants us to share in His divine nature. It is nothing less than the life of the Lord Himself imparted and flowing into our whole beings, so that our very bodies are quickened, so that every tissue, every drop of blood, and our bones, joints, and marrow receive this divine life. I believe that the Lord wants this divine life to flow right into our natural bodies, this *"law of the spirit of life in Christ Jesus"* that makes us *"free from the law of sin and death"* (Rom. 8:2).

God wants to establish our faith so that we will grasp this divine life, this divine nature of the Son of God, in order that our *"spirit, soul, and body* [will] *be* [sanctified completely and] *preserved blameless at the coming of our Lord Jesus Christ"* (1 Thess. 5:23).

When the woman who had suffered for twelve years from a flow of blood was healed, Jesus perceived that power had gone out of Him (Mark 5:25–34). The woman's faith reached out and took hold, and His power was imparted. Immediately, the woman's being was charged with life, and her weakness departed. The conveying of this power produces everything you need, but it comes only as your faith reaches out for its impartation. Faith is the victory. If you can believe, the healing power is yours.

I suffered for many years from hemorrhoids, until my whole body was thoroughly weak; the blood used to gush from me. One day I got desperate, and I took a bottle of oil and anointed myself. I said to the Lord, "Do what You want to, quickly." I was healed at that very moment. God wants us to have an activity of faith that dares to believe God. There is what seems to be faith, an appearance of faith, but real faith believes God right to the end.

What was the difference between Zacharias and Mary? The angel came to Zacharias and told him, *"Your wife Elizabeth will bear you a son"* (Luke 1:13). Zacharias was in the Holy Place, but he began to question this message, saying, *"I am an old man, and my wife is well advanced in years"* (v. 18). Gabriel, the angel of the Lord, rebuked him for his unbelief and told him, *"You will be mute and not able to speak until the day these things take place, because you did not believe my words"* (v. 20).

Note the contrast when the angel came to Mary. She said, *"Behold the maidservant of the Lord! Let it be to me according to your word"* (v. 38).

And Elizabeth greeted Mary with the words, *"Blessed is she who believed, for there will be a fulfillment of those things which were told her from the Lord"* (v. 45).

God wants us to believe His Word in the same way. He wants us to come with a boldness of faith, declaring, "You have promised it, Lord. Now do it." God rejoices when we manifest a faith that holds Him to His Word. Can we get there?

Faith Claims the Victory

The Lord has called us to this *"glory and virtue"* (2 Pet. 1:3). As our faith claims His promises, we will see this evidenced.

I remember one day I was holding a meeting. My uncle came and said, "Aunt Mary would like to see Smith before she dies." I went to see her, and she was assuredly dying.

I said, "Lord, can't You do something?" All I did was stretch out my hands and lay them on her. It seemed as though there was an immediate touch of the glory and power of the Lord.

Aunt Mary cried, "It is going all over my body." That day she was made perfectly whole.

One day I was preaching, and a man brought a boy who was wrapped in bandages. It was impossible for him to walk, so it was difficult for them to get him to the platform. They passed him over about six seats. The power of the Lord was present to heal, and it entered right into the child as I placed my hands on him. The child cried, "Daddy, it is going all over me." They took off the boy's bandages and found nothing wrong with him.

The Lord wants us to be walking letters of His Word. Jesus is the Word and the power in us. It is His desire to work in and through us *"for His good pleasure"* (Phil. 2:13). We must believe that He is in us. There are boundless possibilities for us if we dare to act in God and dare to believe that the wonderful power of our living Christ will be made clear through us as we lay our hands on the sick in His name (Mark 16:18).

The *"exceedingly great and precious promises"* (2 Pet. 1:4) of the Word are given to us that we might be *"partakers of the divine nature"* (v. 4). I feel the Holy Spirit is grieved with us when we know these things but do not do greater deeds for God. Does not the Holy Spirit show us wide-open doors of opportunity? Will we not let God lead us to greater things? Will we not believe God to take us on to greater demonstrations of His power? He calls us to forget the things that are behind, reach toward the things ahead, and *"press toward the goal for the prize of the upward call of God in Christ Jesus"* (Phil. 3:13–14).

9

The Words of This Life

But a certain man named Ananias, with Sapphira his wife, sold a possession. And he kept back part of the proceeds, his wife also being aware of it, and brought a certain part and laid it at the apostles' feet. But Peter said, "Ananias, why has Satan filled your heart to lie to the Holy Spirit and keep back part of the price of the land for yourself? While it remained, was it not your own? And after it was sold, was it not in your own control? Why have you conceived this thing in your heart? You have not lied to men but to God." Then Ananias, hearing these words, fell down and breathed his last. So great fear came upon all those who heard these things. And the young men arose and wrapped him up, carried him out, and buried him. Now it was about three hours later when his wife came in, not knowing what had happened. And Peter answered her, "Tell me whether you sold the land for so much?" She said, "Yes, for so much." Then Peter said to her, "How is it that you have agreed together to test the Spirit of the Lord? Look, the feet of those who have buried your husband are at the door, and they will carry you out." Then immediately she fell down at his feet and breathed her last. And the young men came in and found her dead, and carrying her out, buried her by her husband. So great fear came upon all the church and upon all who heard

these things. And through the hands of the apostles many signs and wonders were done among the people. And they were all with one accord in Solomon's Porch. Yet none of the rest dared join them, but the people esteemed them highly. And believers were increasingly added to the Lord, multitudes of both men and women, so that they brought the sick out into the streets and laid them on beds and couches, that at least the shadow of Peter passing by might fall on some of them. Also a multitude gathered from the surrounding cities to Jerusalem, bringing sick people and those who were tormented by unclean spirits, and they were all healed. Then the high priest rose up, and all those who were with him (which is the sect of the Sadducees), and they were filled with indignation, and laid their hands on the apostles and put them in the common prison. But at night an angel of the Lord opened the prison doors and brought them out, and said, "Go, stand in the temple and speak to the people all the words of this life."
—Acts 5:1–20

Notice this expression that the Lord gives of the gospel message— *"the words of this life."* It is the most wonderful life possible—the life of faith in the Son of God. This is the life where God is present all the time. He is all around, and He is within. It is the life of many revelations and of many manifestations of God's Holy Spirit, a life in which the Lord is continually seen, known, felt, and heard. It is a life without death, for *"we have passed from death to life"* (1 John 3:14). The very life of God has come within us. Where that life is in its fullness, disease cannot exist. It would take me a month to tell what there is in this wonderful life. Everyone can enter in and possess and be possessed by this life.

It is possible for you to be within the vicinity of this life and yet miss it. It is possible for you to be in a place where God is pouring out His Spirit and yet miss the blessing that God is so willing to bestow. This is all due to a lack of revelation and a misunderstanding of the infinite grace of God and of *"the God of all grace"* (1 Pet. 5:10), who is willing to give to all who will reach out the hand of faith. This life that He freely bestows is a gift. Some think they have to earn it, and they miss the whole thing. Oh, for a simple faith to receive all that God so lavishly offers! You can never be ordinary from the day you receive this life from above. You become extraordinary, filled with the extraordinary power of our extraordinary God.

Why Did Ananias and Sapphira Die?

Ananias and Sapphira were in the wonderful revival that God gave to the early church, yet they missed it. They thought that possibly the thing might fail. They wanted to have a reserve for themselves in case it turned out to be a failure.

There are many people like them today. Many people make vows to God in times of great crisis in their lives but fail to keep their vows, and in the end they become spiritually bankrupt. Blessed is the man *"who swears to his own hurt and does not change"* (Ps. 15:4), who keeps the vow he has made to God, who is willing to lay his all at God's feet. The man who does this never becomes a lean soul. God has promised to *"strengthen* [his] *bones"* (Isa. 58:11). There is no dry place for such a man. He is always *"fresh and flourishing"* (Ps. 92:14), and he becomes stronger and stronger. It pays to trust God with all and to hold back nothing.

I wish I could make you see how great a God we have. Ananias and Sapphira were really doubting God and were questioning whether this work that He had begun would go on. They wanted to get some glory for selling their property, but because of their lack of faith, they kept part of the proceeds in reserve in case the work of God were to fail.

Many are doubting whether this Pentecostal revival will go on. Do you think this Pentecostal work will stop? Never. For fifteen years I have been in constant revival, and I am sure that it will never stop.

When George Stephenson built his first engine, he took his sister Mary to see it. She looked at it and said to her brother, "George, it'll never go." He said to her, "Get in, Mary." She said again, "It'll never go." He said to her, "We'll see; you get in." Mary at last got in. The whistle blew, there was a puff and a rattle, and the engine started off. Then Mary cried out, "George, it'll never stop!"

People are looking at this Pentecostal revival, and they are very critical. They are saying, "It'll never go." However, when they are induced to come into the work, they one and all say, "It'll never stop." This revival of God is sweeping on and on, and there is no stopping the current of life, of love, of inspiration, and of power.

Interpretation of Tongues

It is the living Word who has brought this. It is the Lamb in the midst, *"the same yesterday, today, and forever."*

God has brought unlimited resources for everyone. Do not doubt. Hear with the ear of faith. God is in the midst. Make sure that it is God who has set forth what you see and hear today (Acts 2:33).

I want you to see that in the early church, controlled by the power of the Holy Spirit, it was not possible for a lie to exist. The moment it came into the church, there was instant death. Likewise, as the power of the Holy Spirit increases in these days of the latter rain, it will be impossible for any man to remain in our midst with a lying spirit. God will purify the church. The Word of God will be in such power in healing and other spiritual manifestations, that great fear will be upon all those who see these things.

To the natural mind, it seems a small thing for Ananias and Sapphira to want to have a little to fall back on, but I want to tell you that you can please God and get things from God only through a living faith. God never fails. God never can fail.

Our Merciful and Healing God

When I was in Bergen, Norway, a young woman came to the meeting who was employed at the hospital as a nurse. A big cancerous tumor had developed on her nose. The nose was enlarged and had become black and very inflamed.

She came for prayer, and I asked her, "What is your condition?"

She said, "I dare not touch my nose; it gives me so much pain."

I said to all the people, "I want you to look at this nurse and notice her terrible condition. I believe that our God is merciful, that He is faithful, and that He will bring to nothing this condition that the devil has brought about. I am going to curse this disease in the all-powerful name of Jesus. The pain will go. I believe God will give us an exhibition of His grace, and I will ask this young woman to come to the meeting tomorrow night and declare what God has done for her."

Oh, the awfulness of sin! Oh, the awfulness of the power of sin! Oh, the awfulness of the consequences of the Fall! When I see cancer, I always know it is an evil spirit. I can never believe it is otherwise. It is the same way with tumors. Can this be the work of God? May God help me to show you that this is the work of the devil, and to show you the way out.

I do not condemn people who sin. I don't scold people. I know what is behind the sin. I know that the devil is always going about *"like a roaring lion, seeking whom he may devour"* (1 Pet. 5:8). I always remember the patience and love of the Lord Jesus Christ. When they brought to Him a woman whom they had taken in adultery, telling Him that they had caught her in the very act, He simply stooped down and wrote on the ground. Then He quietly said, *"He who is without sin among you, let him throw a stone at her first"* (John 8:7). I have never seen a man without sin. *"All have sinned and fall short of the glory of God"* (Rom. 3:23). But I read in this blessed gospel message that God *"has laid on Him* [Jesus] *the iniquity of us all"* (Isa. 53:6).

When I see an evil condition, I feel that I must stand in my position and rebuke the condition. I laid my hands on the nose of that suffering nurse and cursed the evil power that was causing her so much distress. The next night the place was packed. The people were so jammed together that it seemed as if there was not room for one more to enter that house. How God's rain fell upon us! How good God is, so full of grace and so full of love. I saw the nurse in the audience, and asked her to come forward. She came and showed everyone what God had done. He had perfectly healed her. Oh, I tell you, He is just the same Jesus. He is just the same today (Heb. 13:8). All things are possible if you dare to trust God (Mark 9:23).

Church Growth and Numerous Healings

When the power of God came so mightily upon the early church, even in the death of Ananias and Sapphira, great fear came upon all the people. And when we are in the presence of God, when God is working mightily in our midst, there comes a great fear, a reverence, a holiness of life, a purity that fears to displease God. We read that no man dared to join them, but God *"added to the church...those who were being saved"* (Acts 2:47). I would rather have God add to our Pentecostal church than have all the town join it. God added daily to His own church.

The next thing that happened was that people became so assured that God was working that they knew that anything would be possible, and they brought their sick *"into the streets and laid them on beds and couches, that at least the shadow of Peter passing by might fall on...them."* Multitudes of sick people and those oppressed with evil spirits were brought to the apostles, and God healed every one of them. I do not believe that it was the shadow of Peter that healed them, but the power of God was mightily present, and the faith of the people was so aroused that they joined with one heart to believe God. God will always meet people on the basis of faith.

Revivals in Norway and Ireland

God's tide is rising all over the earth. I had been preaching in Stavanger, Norway, and was very tired and wanted a few hours' rest. I went to my next appointment, arriving at about 9:30 in the morning. My first meeting was to be at night. I said to my interpreter, "After we have had something to eat, let's go down to the fjords."

We spent three or four hours down by the sea and at about 4:30 returned. We found the end of the street, which had a narrow entrance, just filled with automobiles, wagons, and so on, containing invalids and sick people of every kind. I went up to the house and was told that the house was full of sick people, too. It reminded me of the scene described in the fifth chapter of Acts. I began praying for the people in the street, and God began to heal the people. How wonderfully He healed those people who were in the house.

When we sat down for lunch, the telephone rang, and someone at the other end was saying, "What shall we do? The town hall is already full; the police cannot control things."

In that little Norwegian town, the people were jammed together, and oh, how the power of God fell upon us! A cry went up from everyone, "Isn't this the revival?" Revival is coming. The breath of the Almighty is coming. The breath of God shows every defect, and as it comes flowing in like a river, everybody will need a fresh anointing, a fresh cleansing of the blood. You can depend on it that that breath is upon us.

One time I was at a meeting in Ireland. Many sick people were carried to that meeting, and helpless ones were brought there. Many people in that place were seeking the baptism in the Holy Spirit. Some of them had been seeking for years. There were sinners there who were under mighty conviction. A moment came when the breath of God swept through the meeting. In about ten minutes, every sinner in the place was saved.

Everyone who had been seeking the Holy Spirit was baptized, and every sick one was healed. God is a reality, and His power can never fail. As our faith reaches out, God will meet us, and the same rain will fall. It is the same blood that cleanses, the same power, the same Holy Spirit, and the same Jesus made real through the power of the Holy Spirit! What would happen if we would believe God?

Right now, the precious blood of the Lord Jesus Christ is effective to cleanse your heart and put this life, this wonderful life of God, within you. The blood will make you every bit whole if you dare to believe. The Bible is full of entreaty for you to come and partake and receive the grace, the power, the strength, the righteousness, and the full redemption of Jesus Christ. He never fails to hear when we believe.

A Lame Man and His Son

At one place where I was, a lame man was brought to me who had been in bed for two years, with no hope of recovery. He was brought thirty miles to the meeting, and he came up on crutches to be prayed for. His boy was also afflicted in the knees, and they had four crutches between the two of them. The man's face was full of torture. But there is healing power in the Lord, and He never fails to heal when we believe. In the name of Jesus—that name so full of power—I put my hand down that leg that was so diseased. The man threw down his crutches, and all were astonished as they saw him walking up and down without aid. The little boy called out to his father, "Papa, me; papa, me, me, me!" The little boy, who had two withered knees, wanted the same touch. And the same Jesus was there to bring a real deliverance to the little captive. He was completely healed.

These were legs that were touched. If God will stretch out His mighty power to loose afflicted legs, what mercy will He extend to that soul of yours that must exist forever? Hear the Lord say,

> *The Spirit of the LORD is upon Me, because He has anointed Me to preach the gospel to the poor; He has sent Me to heal the brokenhearted, to proclaim liberty to the captives and recovery of sight to the blind, to set at liberty those who are oppressed.* (Luke 4:18)

He invites you, *"Come to Me, all you who labor and are heavy laden, and I will give you rest"* (Matt. 11:28). God is willing in His great mercy to touch your limbs with His mighty, vital power, and if He is willing to do this, how much more eager He is to deliver you from the power of the enemy and to make you a child of the King! How much more necessary it is for you to be healed of your soul sickness than of your bodily ailments! And God is willing to give the double cure.

A Young Man Who Had Fallen into Sin

I was passing through the city of London one time, and Mr. Mundell, the secretary of the Pentecostal Missionary Union, found out that I was there. He arranged for me to meet him at a certain place at 3:30 in the afternoon. I was to meet a certain boy whose father and mother lived in the city of Salisbury. They had sent this young man to London to take care of their business. He had been a leader in Sunday school work, but he had been betrayed and had fallen. Sin is awful, and *"the wages of sin is death"* (Rom. 6:23). Yet, there is another word: *"but the gift of God is eternal life."* This young man was in great distress; he had contracted a horrible disease and was afraid to tell anyone. There was nothing but death ahead for him. When the father and mother found out about his condition, they suffered inexpressible grief.

When we got to the house, Brother Mundell suggested that we begin to pray. I said, "God does not say so. We are not going to pray yet. I want to quote a Scripture: *'Fools, because of their transgression, and because of their iniquities, were afflicted. Their soul abhorred all manner of food, and they drew near to the gates of death'* (Ps. 107:17)."

The young man cried out, "I am that fool." He broke down and told us the story of his fall. Oh, if men would only repent and confess their sins, how God would stretch out His hand to heal and to save! The moment that young man repented, a great abscess burst, and God sent power into his life, giving him a mighty deliverance.

God is gracious and is *"not willing that any should perish"* (2 Pet. 3:9). How many are willing to make a clean break from their sins? I tell you that the moment you do this, God will open heaven. It is an easy thing for Him to save your soul and heal your disease if you will only come and take shelter today in *"the secret place of the Most High"* (Ps. 91:1). He will satisfy you with a long life and show you His salvation (v. 16). *"In [His] presence is fullness of joy; at [His] right hand are pleasures forevermore"* (Ps. 16:11). There is full redemption for all through the precious blood of the Son of God.

✯⊰≕═╪⊱✯

10

Life in the Spirit

*Do we begin again to commend ourselves? Or do we need,
as some others, epistles of commendation to you or letters of
commendation from you? You are our epistle written in our
hearts, known and read by all men; clearly you are an epistle
of Christ, ministered by us, written not with ink but by the
Spirit of the living God, not on tablets of stone but on
tablets of flesh, that is, of the heart. And we have such trust
through Christ toward God. Not that we are sufficient of
ourselves to think of anything as being from ourselves, but
our sufficiency is from God, who also made us sufficient as
ministers of the new covenant, not of the letter but of the
Spirit; for the letter kills, but the Spirit gives life. But if the
ministry of death, written and engraved on stones, was
glorious, so that the children of Israel could not look steadily
at the face of Moses because of the glory of his countenance,
which glory was passing away ["done away" KJV], how will
the ministry of the Spirit not be more glorious? For if the
ministry of condemnation had glory, the ministry of
righteousness exceeds much more in glory. For even what
was made glorious had no glory in this respect, because of
the glory that excels. For if what is passing away ["done
away" KJV] was glorious, what remains is much more
glorious. Therefore, since we have such hope, we use great
boldness of speech; unlike Moses, who put a veil over his*

119

face so that the children of Israel could not look steadily at
the end of what was passing away. But their minds were
blinded. For until this day the same veil remains unlifted in
the reading of the Old Testament, because the veil is taken
away ["done away" KJV] in Christ. But even to this day,
when Moses is read, a veil lies on their heart. Nevertheless
when one turns to the Lord, the veil is taken away. Now the
Lord is the Spirit; and where the Spirit of the Lord is, there is
liberty. But we all, with unveiled face, beholding as in a
mirror the glory of the Lord, are being transformed into
the same image from glory to glory, just
as by the Spirit of the Lord.
—2 Corinthians 3

We are told in Hebrews 6:1–2 that we are to leave the first principles of the doctrine of Christ and go on to perfection, not laying again the foundation of repentance from dead works and the doctrine of baptisms and the other first principles. What would you think of a builder who was continually pulling down his house and putting in fresh foundations? Never look back if you want the power of God in your life. You will find out that in the measure you have allowed yourself to look back, you have missed what God had for you.

The Holy Spirit shows us that we must never look back to the law of sin and death from which we have been delivered. (See Romans 8:2.) God has brought us into a new order of things, a life of love and liberty in Christ Jesus that is beyond all human comprehension. Many are brought into this new life through the power of the Spirit of God, and then, like the Galatians, who ran well at the beginning, they try to perfect themselves through legalism. (See Galatians 3:1–3; 5:7.) They turn back from a life in the Spirit to a life along natural lines. God is not pleased with this, for He has no place for the person who has lost the vision. The only thing to do is to repent. Don't try to cover up anything. If you have been tripped up in any area, confess it; then look to God to bring you to a place of stability of faith where your whole walk will be in the Spirit.

The Joy of Being God's Child

We all ought to have a clear conviction that *"salvation is of the LORD"* (Jonah 2:9). Salvation is more than a human order of things. If the enemy can move you from a place of faith, he can get you outside of the plan of God. The moment a man falls into sin, divine life ceases to flow, and his life becomes one of helplessness. But this is not God's plan for any of His children.

Read the third chapter of John's first epistle, and take your place as a child of God. Take the place of knowing that you are a child of God, and remember that as your hope is set in Christ, it should have a purifying effect on your life. The Holy Spirit says, *"Whoever has been born of God does not sin, for His seed remains in him; and he cannot sin, because he has been born of God"* (1 John 3:9). There is life and power in the seed of the Word that is implanted within. God is in that *"cannot,"* and there is more power in that word of His than in any human objections. God's thought for every one of us is that we will reign in life by Jesus Christ (Rom. 5:17). You must come to see how wonderful you are in God and how helpless you are in yourself.

God declared Himself to be mightier than every opposing power when He cast out the powers of darkness from heaven. I want you to know that the same power that cast the devil out of heaven dwells in every person who is born of God. If you would only realize this, you would *"reign in life"* (Rom. 5:17). When you see people laid out under an evil power, when you see the powers of evil manifesting themselves, always ask them the question, "Did Jesus come in the flesh?" I have never heard an evil power answer in the affirmative. (See 1 John 4:2–3.) When you know you have an evil spirit to deal with, you have power to cast it out. Believe this fact, and act on it, for *"greater is he that is in you, than he that is in the world"* (1 John 4:4 KJV). God intends for you to overcome and has put a force within you whereby you may defeat the devil.

Triumphing in Trials

Temptations will come to all. If you are not worth tempting, you are not worth much. Job said, *"When He has tested me, I shall come forth as gold"* (Job 23:10). In every temptation that comes, the Lord allows you to be tempted to the very hilt, but He will never allow you to be defeated if you walk in obedience. Right in the midst of the temptation, He will always *"make the way of escape"* (1 Cor. 10:13).

Interpretation of Tongues

God comes forth and with His power sweeps away the refuge of lies and all the powers of darkness and causes you always to triumph in Christ Jesus. The Lord loves His saints and covers them with His almighty wings.

May God help us to see this truth. We cannot be *"to the praise of His glory"* (Eph. 1:12) until we are ready for trials and are able to triumph in them. We cannot get away from the fact that sin came in by nature, but God comes into our nature and puts sin into the place of death. Why? So that the Spirit of God may come into the temple in all His power and liberty, and so that right here in this present, evil world, the devil may be dethroned by the believer.

The Spirit's Work in Our Hearts

Satan is always endeavoring to bring the saints of God into disrepute by bringing against them slanderous accusations, but the Holy Spirit never comes with condemnation. He always reveals the blood of Christ. He always brings us help. The Lord Jesus referred to Him as the Comforter who would come (John 14:16 KJV). He is always on hand to help in the seasons of testing and trial. The Holy Spirit is the lifting power of the church of Christ.

Paul told us that we are *"clearly...an epistle of Christ ...written not with ink but by the Spirit of the living God, not on tablets of stone but on tablets of flesh, that is, of the heart."* The Holy Spirit begins in the heart, right in the depths of human affections. He brings into the heart the riches of the revelation of Christ, implanting a purity and holiness there, so that out of the depths of the heart, praises may well up continually.

The Holy Spirit will make us epistles of Christ, ever proclaiming that Jesus our Lord is our Redeemer and that He is ever before God as a slain Lamb. God has never set aside that revelation. Because of the perfect atonement of that slain Lamb, there is salvation, healing, and deliverance for all. Some people think that they have to be cleansed only once, but as we walk in the light, the blood of Jesus Christ is ever cleansing us (1 John 1:7).

The very life of Christ has been put within us and is moving within us—a perfect life. May the Lord help us to see the power of this life. The days of a man's life are seventy years (Ps. 90:10). And so, in the natural order of things, my life will be finished in seven years, but I have begun a new life that will never end. *"From everlasting to everlasting, You are God"* (v. 2). This is the life I have come into, and there is no end to this life. In me is working a power that is stronger than every other power. Christ, the power of God, is formed within me. I can see why we need to be clothed from above, for the life within me is a thousand times bigger than I am outside. There must be a tremendous expansion. I see, and cannot help seeing, that this life cannot be understood in the natural. No natural reason can comprehend the divine plan.

Our All-Sufficient God

We are not *"sufficient of ourselves to think of anything as being from ourselves, but our sufficiency is from God."* We leave the old order of things. If we go back, we miss the plan. We can never have confidence in the flesh (Phil. 3:3); we cannot touch that. We are in a new order, a spiritual order. It is a new life of absolute faith in our God's sufficiency in everything that pertains to *"life and godliness"* (2 Pet. 1:3).

You could never come into this place and be a Seventh-day Adventist, for the law has no place in you. You are set free from it. At the same time, like Paul, you are bound in the Spirit (Acts 20:22) so that you would not do anything to grieve the Lord.

Paul further told us that God has *"made us sufficient as ministers of the new covenant, not of the letter but of the Spirit; for the letter kills, but the Spirit gives life.* " It is one thing to read this and another thing to have the revelation of it and to see the spiritual force of it. Any man can live in the letter and become dry and wordy, limited in knowledge of spiritual truths and spending all his time splitting hairs. But as soon as he touches the realm of the Spirit, all the dryness goes; the spirit of criticism leaves. There can be no divisions in a life in the Spirit. The Spirit of God brings such pliability and such love! There is no love like the love in the Spirit. It is a pure, holy, divine love that is poured out in our hearts by the Spirit (Rom. 5:5). It loves to serve and to honor the Lord.

The Holy Spirit's Life-Changing Power

I can never estimate what the baptism in the Holy Spirit has meant to me these past fifteen years. It seems as if every year has had three years packed into it, so that I feel as if I have had forty-five years of happy service since 1907. Life is getting better all the time. It is a luxury to be filled with the Spirit, and at the same time it is a divine command for us: *"Do not be drunk with wine, in which is dissipation; but be filled with the Spirit"* (Eph. 5:18). No Pentecostal person ought to get out of bed without being lost in the Spirit and speaking in tongues as the Spirit gives utterance. No one should come through the door of the church without speaking in tongues or having a psalm or a note of praise (1 Cor. 14:26).

Regarding the incoming of the Spirit, I emphasize that He should so fill us that every member in the body is yielded to Him. I also emphasize that no one is baptized in the Spirit without speaking in tongues as the

Spirit gives utterance. I maintain that with a constant filling, you will speak in tongues morning, noon, and night. As you live in the Spirit, when you walk down the steps of your house, the devil will have to flee before you. You will be more than a conqueror over the devil (Rom. 8:37).

I see everything as a failure except what is done in the Spirit. But as you live in the Spirit, you move, act, eat, drink, and do everything to the glory of God (1 Cor. 10:31). Our message is always this: *"Be filled with the Spirit."* This is God's place for you, and it is as far above the natural life as the heavens are above the earth. Yield yourself so that God will fill you.

The Wonderful New Covenant

The Israelites tried Moses tremendously. They were always in trouble. But as he went up onto the mountain and God unfolded to him the Ten Commandments, the glory fell. He rejoiced to bring those two tablets of stone down from the mountain, and his very face shone with the glory. He was bringing to Israel that which, if obeyed, would bring life.

I think of my Lord coming from heaven. I think all heaven was moved by the sight. The letter of the law was brought by Moses, and it was made glorious, but all its glory was dimmed before the excelling glory that Jesus brought to us in the Spirit of life. The glory of Sinai paled before the glory of Pentecost. Those tablets of stone with their "Thou shalt not's" are done away with, for they never brought life to anyone. The Lord has brought in a new covenant, putting His law in our minds and writing it in our hearts (Jer. 31:33)—this new *"law of the Spirit of life"* (Rom. 8:2). As the Holy Spirit comes in, He fills us with such love and liberty that we shout for joy, "Done away! Done away!" (See 2 Corinthians 3:11 KJV.) Henceforth, there is a new cry in our hearts: *"I delight to do Your will, O my God"* (Ps. 40:8). *"He takes away the first that He may establish the second"* (Heb. 10:9). In other words, He takes away *"the ministry of death, written and engraved on stones,"* so that He may establish *"the ministry of righteousness,"* this life in the Spirit.

You ask, "Does a man who is filled with the Spirit cease to keep the commandments?" I simply repeat what the Spirit of God has told us here, that this *"ministry of death, written and engraved on stones"* (and you know that the Ten Commandments were written on stones) is *"done away* [with] *"* (2 Cor. 3:11 KJV). The man who becomes a living epistle of Christ, written by the Spirit of the living God, has ceased to be an adulterer or a murderer or a covetous man; the will of God is his delight. I love to do the will of God; there is no irksomeness to it. It is no trial to pray, no trouble to read the Word of God; it is not a hard thing to go to the place of worship. With the psalmist I say, *"I was glad when they said to me, 'Let us go into the house of the LORD'"* (Ps. 122:1).

How does this new life work out? It works out because God *"works in you both to will and to do for His good pleasure"* (Phil. 2:13). There is a big difference between a pump and a spring. The law is a pump; the baptism in the Holy Spirit is a spring. The old pump gets out of order; the parts wear out, and the well runs dry. *"The letter kills."* But the spring is ever bubbling up, and there is a ceaseless flow direct from the throne of God. There is life.

It is written of Christ, *"You love righteousness and hate wickedness"* (Ps. 45:7). In this new life in the Spirit, in this new covenant life, you love the things that are

right and pure and holy, and you shudder at all things
that are wrong. Jesus was able to say, *"The ruler of this
world is coming, and he has nothing in Me"* (John
14:30), and the moment we are filled with the Spirit of
God, we are brought into a wonderful condition like this.
Furthermore, as we continue to be filled with the Spirit,
the enemy cannot have an inch of territory in us.

How to Bring Conviction of Sin

Don't you believe that you can be so filled with the
Spirit that a person who is not living right can be judged
and convicted by your presence? As we go on in the life
of the Spirit, it will be said of us, *"In whose eyes a vile
person is despised"* (Ps. 15:4). Jesus lived in this realm
and moved in it, and His life was a constant reproof to
the wickedness around Him. "But He was the Son of
God," you say. God, through Him, has brought us into
the place of sonship, and I believe that if the Holy Spirit
has a chance at us, He can make something of us and
bring us to the same place.

I don't want to boast. If I glory in anything, it is only
in the Lord, who has been so gracious to me (1 Cor.
1:31). But I remember one time stepping out of a railway
coach to wash my hands. I had a season of prayer, and
the Lord just filled me to overflowing with His love. I was
going to a convention in Ireland, and I could not get
there fast enough. As I returned to my seat, I believe that
the Spirit of the Lord was so heavy upon me that my
face must have shone. (When the Spirit transforms a
man's very countenance, he cannot tell this on his own.)
There were two clerical men sitting together, and as I got
into the coach again, one of them cried out, "You convict me of sin." Within three minutes everyone in the

coach was crying to God for salvation. This has happened many times in my life. It is the *"ministry of the Spirit"* that Paul spoke of. This filling of the Spirit will make your life effective, so that even the people in the stores where you shop will want to leave your presence because they are brought under conviction.

We must move away from everything that pertains to the letter. All that we do must be done under the anointing of the Spirit. Our problem has been that we as Pentecostal people have been living in the letter. Believe what the Holy Spirit said through Paul—that this entire *"ministry of condemnation"* that has hindered your liberty in Christ is done away with. The law has been done away with! As far as you are concerned, that old order of things is forever done away with, and the Spirit of God has brought in a new life of purity and love. The Holy Spirit takes it for granted that you are finished with all the things of the old life when you become a new creation in Christ. In the life in the Spirit, the old allurements have lost their power. Satan will meet you at every turn, but the Spirit of God will always *"lift up a standard against him"* (Isa. 59:19).

Oh, if God had His way, we would be like torches, purifying the very atmosphere wherever we go, moving back the forces of wickedness.

Interpretation of Tongues
"The Lord is that Spirit." He moves in your heart. He shows you that the power within you is mightier than all the powers of darkness.

What do I mean when I say that the law has been done away with? Do I mean that you will be disloyal? No, you will be more than loyal. Will you grumble when you are treated badly? No, you will turn the other cheek (Matt. 5:39). You will always do this when God lives in you. Leave yourself in God's hands. Enter into rest. *"For he who has entered His rest has himself also ceased from his works as God did from His"* (Heb. 4:10). Oh, this is a lovely rest! The whole life is a Sabbath. This is the only life that can glorify God. It is a life of joy, and every day is a day of heaven on earth.

Daily Transformation

There is a continual transformation in this life. Beholding the Lord and His glory, we are *"transformed into the same image from glory to glory, just as by the Spirit of the Lord."* There is a continual unveiling, a constant revelation, a repeated clothing from above. I want you to promise God never to look back, never to go back to what the Spirit has said is done away with. I promised the Lord that I would never allow myself to doubt His Word.

There is one thing about a baby: he takes all that comes to him. A so-called prudent man lets his reason cheat him out of God's best, but a baby takes all the milk his mother brings and even tries to swallow the bottle. The baby can't walk, but the mother carries him; the baby can't dress himself, but the mother dresses him. The baby can't even talk. Similarly, in the life of the Spirit, God undertakes to do what we cannot do. We are carried along by Him. He clothes us, and He gives us utterance. Oh, that we all had the simplicity of babes!

II

What It Means to Be Full of the Holy Spirit

And in those days, when the number of the disciples was multiplied, there arose a murmuring of the Grecians against the Hebrews, because their widows were neglected in the daily ministration. Then the twelve called the multitude of the disciples unto them, and said, It is not reason that we should leave the word of God, and serve tables. Wherefore, brethren, look ye out among you seven men of honest report, full of the Holy Ghost and wisdom, whom we may appoint over this business. But we will give ourselves continually to prayer, and to the ministry of the word. And the saying pleased the whole multitude: and they chose Stephen, a man full of faith and of the Holy Ghost, and Philip, and Prochorus, and Nicanor, and Timon, and Parmenas, and Nicolas a proselyte of Antioch: Whom they set before the apostles: and when they had prayed, they laid their hands on them. And the word of God increased; and the number of the disciples multiplied in Jerusalem greatly; and a great company of the priests were obedient to the faith. And Stephen, full of faith and power, did great wonders and miracles among the people. Then there arose certain of the synagogue, which is called the synagogue of the Libertines, and Cyrenians, and Alexandrians, and of them of Cilicia

*and of Asia, disputing with Stephen. And they were not
able to resist the wisdom and the spirit by which he spake.
Then they suborned men, which said, We have heard him
speak blasphemous words against Moses, and against God.
And they stirred up the people, and the elders, and the
scribes, and came upon him, and caught him, and brought
him to the council, and set up false witnesses, which said,
This man ceaseth not to speak blasphemous words against
this holy place, and the law: for we have heard him say, that
this Jesus of Nazareth shall destroy this place, and shall
change the customs which Moses delivered us. And all that
sat in the council, looking stedfastly on him, saw his face as
it had been the face of an angel.*
—Acts 6

I n the days when the number of disciples began to
multiply, there arose a situation in which the Twelve
had to make a definite decision not to occupy themselves with serving tables, but to give themselves continually to prayer and to the ministry of the Word. How
important it is for all God's ministers to be continually in
prayer and constantly feeding on the Scriptures of Truth.
I often offer a reward to anyone who can catch me anywhere without my Bible or my New Testament.

None of you can be strong in God unless you are
diligently and constantly listening to what God has to say
to you through His Word. You cannot know the power
and the nature of God unless you partake of His in-
breathed Word. Read it in the morning, in the evening,
and at every opportunity you get. After every meal, instead of indulging in unprofitable conversation around
the table, read a chapter from the Word, and then have
a season of prayer. I endeavor to make a point of doing
this no matter where or with whom I am staying.

The psalmist said that he had hidden God's Word in his heart so that he might not sin against Him (Ps. 119:11). You will find that the more of God's Word you hide in your heart, the easier it is to live a holy life. He also testified that God's Word had given him life (v. 50). As you receive God's Word, your whole physical being will be given life, and you will be made strong. As you receive the Word with meekness (James 1:21), you will find faith springing up within yourself. You will have life through the Word.

A Better Plan for You

The Twelve told the rest of the disciples to find seven men to look after the business side of things. They were to be men with a good reputation and filled with the Holy Spirit. Those who were chosen were just ordinary men, but they were filled with the Holy Spirit, and this infilling always lifts a man to a plane above the ordinary. It does not take a cultured or an educated man to fill a position in God's church. What God requires is a yielded, consecrated, holy life, and He can make it a flame of fire. He can baptize *"with the Holy Spirit and fire"* (Matt. 3:11)!

The multitude chose seven men to serve tables. Undoubtedly, they were faithful in their appointed tasks, but we can see that God soon had a better plan for two of them—Philip and Stephen. Philip was so full of the Holy Spirit that he could have a revival wherever God put him down. (See Acts 8:5–8, 26–40.) Man chose him to serve tables, but God chose him to win souls.

Oh, if I could only stir you up to see that, as you are faithful in the humblest role, God can fill you with His Spirit, make you a chosen vessel for Himself, and promote you to a place of mighty ministry in the salvation of souls and in the healing of the sick! Nothing is impossible to a man filled with the Holy Spirit. The possibilities are beyond all human comprehension. When you are filled with the power of the Spirit, God will wonderfully work wherever you go.

When you are filled with the Spirit, you will know the voice of God. I want to give you one illustration of this. When I was going to Australia recently, our boat stopped at Aden and Bombay. In Aden the people came around the ship selling their wares—beautiful carpets and all sorts of Oriental things. There was one man selling some ostrich feathers. As I was looking over the side of the ship watching the trading, a gentleman said to me, "Would you join me in buying that bunch of feathers?" What did I want with feathers? I had no use for such things and no room for them, either. But the gentleman asked me again, "Will you join me in buying that bunch?"

The Spirit of God said to me, "Do it."

The feathers were sold to us for three pounds, and the gentleman said, "I have no money on me, but if you will pay the man for them, I will send the cash down to you by the steward." I paid for the feathers and gave the gentleman his share.

He was traveling first class, and I was traveling second class. I said to him, "No, please don't give that money to the steward. I want you to bring it to me personally in my cabin."

I asked the Lord, "What about these feathers?" He showed me that He had a purpose in my buying them.

At about ten o'clock, the gentleman came to my cabin and said, "I've brought the money."

I said to him, "It is not your money that I want; it is your soul that I am seeking for God." Right there he opened up the whole story of his life and began to seek

God, and that morning he wept his way through to God's salvation.

You have no idea what God can do through you when you are filled with His Spirit. Every day and every hour you can have the divine leading of God. To be filled with the Holy Spirit is great in every respect. I have seen some who had been suffering for years, but when they have been filled with the Holy Spirit, every bit of their sickness has passed away. The Spirit of God has made real to them the life of Jesus, and they have been completely liberated from every sickness and infirmity.

Look at Stephen. He was just an ordinary man chosen to serve tables. But the Holy Spirit was in him, and he was *"full of faith and power"*; therefore, he did great wonders and miracles among the people. There was no resisting *"the wisdom and the Spirit by which he spoke."* How important it is that every man be filled with the Spirit.

Interpretation of Tongues

The divine will is that you should be filled with God; for the power of the Spirit to fill you with the mightiness of God. There is nothing God will withhold from a man filled with the Holy Spirit.

I want to impress the importance of this upon you. It is not healing that I am presenting to you—it is the living Christ. It is a glorious fact that the Son of God came down to bring *"liberty to the captives"* (Luke 4:18).

The Blessing of Persecution

How is it that the moment you are filled with the Holy Spirit persecution starts? It was so with the Lord Jesus Himself. We do not read of any persecution before

135

the Holy Spirit came down upon Him like a dove.
Shortly after this, we find that after He preached in His
hometown, the people wanted to throw Him over the
brow of a hill. (See Luke 4:16–30.) It was the same way
with the twelve disciples. They had no persecution before the Day of Pentecost, but after they were filled with
the Spirit, they were soon in prison.

Satan and the priests of religion will always get
stirred up when a man is filled with the Spirit and does
things in the power of the Spirit. Nevertheless, persecution is the greatest blessing to a church. When we have
persecution, we have purity. If you desire to be filled with
the Spirit, you can count on one thing, and that is persecution. The Lord came to bring division (Luke 12:51),
and even in your own household you may find *"three
against two"* (v. 52).

The Lord Jesus came to bring peace, but soon after
you have peace within, you get persecution without. If
you remain stationary, the devil and his agents will not
disturb you much. But when you press on and go the
whole length with God, the enemy has you as a target.
Nevertheless, God will vindicate you in the midst of the
whole thing.

At a meeting I was holding, the Lord was working,
and many were being healed. A man saw what was taking place and remarked, "I'd like to try this thing." He
came up for prayer and told me that his body was broken in two places.

I laid my hands on him in the name of the Lord and
said to him, "Now, believe God."

The next night he was at the meeting, and he got up
like a lion. He said, "I want to tell you people that this
man here is deceiving you. He laid his hands on me last
night for a rupture in two places, but I'm not a bit better."

I stopped him and said, "You are healed; your trouble is that you won't believe it."

He was at the meeting the next night, and when there was opportunity for testimonies, this man arose. He said, "I'm a mason by trade. Today I was working with a laborer, and he had to put a big stone in place. I helped him and did not feel any pain. I said to myself, 'How did I do that?' I went to a private place where I could take off my clothes, and I found that I was healed."

I told the people, "Last night this man was against the Word of God, but now he believes it. It is true that *'these signs will follow those who believe:...they will lay hands on the sick, and they will recover'* (Mark 16:17–18). Healing is through the power that is in the name of Christ." It is the Spirit who has come to reveal the Word of God and to make it spirit and life to us (John 6:63).

Those of you who are seeking the baptism in the Holy Spirit are entering a place where you will have persecution. Your best friends will leave you—or those you may think are your best friends. No truly good friend will ever leave you. But be assured that your seeking is worthwhile. You will enter into a realm of illumination, a realm of revelation by the power of the Holy Spirit. He reveals the preciousness and the power of the blood of Christ. I have found by the revelation of the Spirit that there is not one thing in me that the blood does not cleanse (1 John 1:9). I have found that God sanctifies me by the blood and reveals the effectiveness of His work by the Spirit.

Life in the Spirit

Stephen was just an ordinary man, but he was clothed with the divine. He was *"full of faith and power,"* and great wonders and miracles were done by him. Oh, this life in the Holy Spirit! Oh, this life of deep inward revelation, of transformation from one state to another, of growing in grace, in all knowledge, and in the power of the Spirit. In this state, the life and the mind of Christ are renewed in you, and He gives constant revelations of the might of His power. It is only this kind of thing that will enable us to stand.

In this life, the Lord puts you in all sorts of places and then reveals His power. I had been preaching in New York, and one day I sailed for England on the *Lusitania*. As soon as I got on board, I went down to my cabin. Two men were there, and one of them said, "Well, will I do for company?" He took out a bottle and poured a glass of whiskey and drank it, and then he filled it up for me.

"I never touch that stuff," I said.

"How can you live without it?" he asked.

"How could I live with it?" I asked.

He admitted, "I have been under the influence of this stuff for months, and they say my insides are all shriveled up. I know that I am dying. I wish I could be delivered, but I just have to keep on drinking. Oh, if I could only be delivered! My father died in England and has given me his fortune, but what good will it be to me except to hasten me to my grave?"

I said to this man, "Say the word, and you will be delivered."

He asked, "What do you mean?"

I said, "Say the word—show that you are willing to be delivered—and God will deliver you."

But it was just as if I had been talking to this platform for all the understanding he showed. I said to him, "Stand still," and I laid my hands on his head in the name of Jesus and cursed that alcohol demon that was taking his life.

He cried out, "I'm free! I'm free! I know I'm free!" He took two bottles of whiskey and threw them overboard, and God saved, sobered, and healed him. I was preaching all the way across the ocean. He sat beside me at the table. Previous to this, he had not been able to eat, but now at every meal he went right through the menu.

You need only a touch from Jesus to have a good time. The power of God is just the same today. To me, He's lovely. To me, He's saving health. To me, He's the Lily of the Valley. Oh, this blessed Nazarene, this King of Kings! Hallelujah!

Will you let Him have your will? Will you let Him have you? If so, all His power is at your disposal.

It's Worth It!

Those who disputed with Stephen *"were not able to resist the wisdom and the Spirit by which he spoke."* Full of rage, they brought him to the council. However, God filled his face with a ray of heaven's light.

Being filled with the Spirit is worthwhile, no matter what it costs. Read in Acts 7 the mighty prophetic utterance by this holy man. Without fear he told them, *"You stiffnecked and uncircumcised in heart and ears! You always resist the Holy Spirit"* (Acts 7:51). When his enemies heard these things, *"they were cut to the heart"* (v. 54). There are two ways of being cut to the heart. Here they gnashed at him with their teeth, cast him out of the city, and stoned him. On the Day of Pentecost, when the people were cut to the heart, they cried out, *"What shall we do?"* (Acts 2:37). They responded in the opposite way.

139

Satan, if he can have his way, will cause you to commit murder. If Jesus has His way, you will repent.

Stephen, full of the Holy Spirit, looked up stead-fastly into heaven and saw the glory of God and the Son of Man standing on the right hand of God. Oh, this being full of the Holy Spirit! How much it means! I was riding for sixty miles one summer day, and as I looked up at the heavens, I had an open vision of Jesus all the way. It takes the Holy Spirit to give this.

Stephen cried out, *"Lord, do not charge them with this sin"* (Acts 7:60). Since he was full of the Spirit, he was full of love. He manifested the very same compassion for his enemies that Jesus did at Calvary.

This being filled with the Holy Spirit is great in every respect. It means constant filling, quickening, and a new life continually. Oh, it's lovely! We have a wonderful Gospel and a great Savior! If you will only be filled with the Holy Spirit, you will have a constant spring within. Yes, as your faith centers on the Lord Jesus, from within you *"will flow rivers of living water"* (John 7:38).

12

Biblical Evidence
of the Baptism

*When the Day of Pentecost had fully come, they were all
with one accord in one place. And suddenly there came a
sound from heaven, as of a rushing mighty wind, and it filled
the whole house where they were sitting. Then there
appeared to them divided tongues, as of fire, and one sat
upon each of them. And they were all filled with the Holy
Spirit and began to speak with other tongues, as the Spirit
gave them utterance. And there were dwelling in Jerusalem
Jews, devout men, from every nation under heaven. And
when this sound occurred, the multitude came together, and
were confused, because everyone heard them speak in his
own language. Then they were all amazed and marveled,
saying to one another, "Look, are not all these who speak
Galileans? And how is it that we hear, each in our own
language in which we were born? Parthians and Medes and
Elamites, those dwelling in Mesopotamia, Judea and
Cappadocia, Pontus and Asia, Phrygia and Pamphylia,
Egypt and the parts of Libya adjoining Cyrene, visitors from
Rome, both Jews and proselytes, Cretans and Arabs; we
hear them speaking in our own tongues the wonderful works
of God." So they were all amazed and perplexed, saying to*

*one another, "Whatever could this mean?" Others mocking
said, "They are full of new wine." But Peter, standing up
with the eleven, raised his voice and said to them, "Men of
Judea and all who dwell in Jerusalem, let this be known to
you, and heed my words. For these are not drunk, as you
suppose, since it is only the third hour of the day.
But this is what was spoken by the prophet Joel:
'And it shall come to pass in the last days, says God,
that I will pour out of My Spirit on all flesh; your sons and
your daughters shall prophesy, your young men shall see
visions, your old men shall dream dreams.'"*
—Acts 2:1–17

*But the manifestation of the Spirit is given to each one for
the profit of all: for to one is given...different kinds of
tongues, to another the interpretation of tongues. But one
and the same Spirit works all these things, distributing to
each one individually as He wills.*
—1 Corinthians 12:7–8, 10–11

There is much controversy today regarding the genuineness of this Pentecostal work. However, there is nothing so convincing as the fact that over fifteen years ago, a revival on Holy Spirit lines began and has never ceased. You will find that in every region throughout the world, God has poured out His Spirit in a remarkable way, in a manner parallel to the glorious revival that inaugurated the church of the first century. People who could not understand what God was doing when He kept them concentrated in prayer, wondered as these days were being brought about by the Holy Spirit, and they found themselves in exactly the same place and entering into an identical experience as the apostles on the Day of Pentecost.

Biblical Evidence of the Baptism

Our Lord Jesus said to His disciples, *"Behold, I send the Promise of My Father upon you; but tarry in the city of Jerusalem until you are endued with power from on high"* (Luke 24:49). God promised through the prophet Joel, *"I will pour out My Spirit on all flesh....On My menservants and on My maidservants I will pour out My Spirit in those days"* (Joel 2:28–29). As there is a widespread misconception concerning this receiving of the Holy Spirit, I believe the Lord would have us examine the Scriptures on this subject.

Tongues and the Baptism

Let me tell you about my own experience of being baptized with the Holy Spirit. You know, beloved, that it had to be something that was based on solid facts in order to move me. I was as certain as possible that I had received the Holy Spirit, and I was absolutely rigid in this conviction. When this Pentecostal outpouring began in England, I went to Sunderland and met with the people who had assembled for the purpose of receiving the Holy Spirit. I was continuously in those meetings causing disturbances, until the people wished I had never come. They said that I was disrupting the conditions for people to receive the baptism. But I was hungry and thirsty for God, and I had gone to Sunderland because I had heard that God was pouring out His Spirit in a new way. I had heard that God had now visited His people and manifested His power, and that people were speaking in tongues as on the Day of Pentecost.

Thus, when I first got to Sunderland, I said to the people, "I cannot understand this meeting. I have left a meeting in Bradford all on fire for God. The fire fell last night, and we were all laid out under the power of God. I

143

have come here for tongues, and I don't hear them—I don't hear anything."

"Oh!" they said. "When you get baptized with the Holy Spirit, you will speak in tongues."

"Oh, is that it?" I said. "When the presence of God came upon me, my tongue was loosened, and when I went in the open air to preach, I really felt that I had a new tongue."

"Ah, no," they said, "that is not it."

"What is it, then?" I asked.

"When you get baptized in the Holy Spirit—"

"I am baptized," I interjected, "and there is no one here who can persuade me that I am not baptized."

So I was up against them, and they were up against me.

I remember a man getting up and saying, "You know, brothers and sisters, I was here three weeks and then the Lord baptized me with the Holy Spirit, and I began to speak with other tongues."

I said, "Let us hear it. That's what I'm here for."

But he could not speak in tongues. I was doing what others are doing today, confusing the twelfth chapter of 1 Corinthians with the second chapter of Acts. These two chapters deal with different things; one deals with the gifts of the Spirit, and the other deals with the baptism of the Spirit with the accompanying sign of tongues. I did not understand this, and so I said to the man, "Let's hear you speak in tongues." But he could not. He had not received the gift of tongues, but the baptism in the Holy Spirit.

As the days passed, I became more and more hungry for God. I had opposed the meetings so much, but the Lord was gracious, and I will always remember that last day—the day I was to leave. God was with me so much. They were to have a meeting, and I went, but I could not be still. This revival was taking place at an Episcopal church. I went to the rectory to say good-bye, and there in the library, I said to Mrs. Boddy, the rector's wife, "I cannot rest any longer; I must have these tongues now."

She replied, "Brother Wigglesworth, it is not the tongues you need but the baptism. If you will allow God to baptize you, the other will be all right."

I answered, "My dear sister, I know I am baptized. You know that I have to leave here at four o'clock. Please lay hands on me so that I may receive the tongues."

She stood up and laid her hands on me, and the fire fell on me.

I said, "The fire's falling." There came a persistent knock at the door, and she had to go out. That was the best thing that could have happened, for I was alone with God.

Then He gave me a revelation. Oh, it was wonderful! He showed me an empty cross and Jesus glorified. I do thank God that the cross is empty, that Christ is no longer on the cross. It was there that He bore the curse, for it is written, *"Cursed is everyone who hangs on a tree"* (Gal. 3:13; see Deuteronomy 21:23). He became *"sin for us, that we might become the righteousness of God in Him"* (2 Cor. 5:21). And now, there He is in the glory.

Then I saw that God had purified me. It seemed that God gave me a new vision, and I saw a perfect being within me, with mouth open, saying, "Clean! Clean! Clean!" When I began to repeat it, I found myself speaking in other tongues. The joy was so great that, when I went to utter it, my tongue failed, and I began to worship God in other tongues *"as the Spirit gave* [me] *utterance"* (Acts 2:4).

It was all as beautiful and peaceful as when Jesus said, *"Peace, be still!"* (Mark 4:39). The tranquillity and the joy of that moment surpassed anything I had ever known up to that time. But, hallelujah, these days have grown with greater, mightier, more wonderful divine manifestations and power! That was only the beginning. There is no end to this kind of beginning. You will never come to the end of the Holy Spirit until you have arrived in glory—until you are right in the presence of God forever—and even then we will always be conscious of His presence.

What had I received? I had received the biblical evidence. This biblical evidence is wonderful to me. I knew I had received the very evidence of the Spirit's incoming that the apostles had received on the Day of Pentecost. I knew that everything I had had up to that time was in the nature of an anointing, bringing me in line with God in preparation. However, now I knew I had the biblical baptism in the Spirit. It had the backing of the Scriptures. You are always right when you have the backing of the Scriptures, and you are never right if you do not have a foundation for your testimony in the Word of God.

For many years, I have thrown out a challenge to any person who can prove to me that he has the baptism without the speaking in tongues as the Spirit gives utterance—to prove it by the Word that he has been baptized in the Holy Spirit without the biblical evidence—but so far, no one has accepted the challenge. I only say this because so many are like I was; they have a rigid idea that they have received the baptism, without having the biblical evidence. The Lord Jesus wants those who preach the Word to have the Word in evidence. Don't be

misled by anything else. Have a biblical proof for everything you have, and then you will be in a place where no
man can move you.

I was so full of joy that I wired home to say that I
had received the Holy Spirit.

As soon as I got home, my boy came running up to
me and said, "Father, have you received the Holy
Spirit?"

I said, "Yes, my boy."

He said, "Let's hear you speak in tongues."

But I could not. Why? I had received the baptism in
the Spirit with the speaking in tongues as the biblical evidence, according to Acts 2:4, but had not received the
gift of tongues according to 1 Corinthians 12. I had received the Giver of all gifts.

Some time later, when I was helping some souls to
seek and receive the baptism of the Spirit, God gave me
the gift of tongues so that I could speak them at any
time. I can speak them, but I will not speak them at just
any time—no, never! I must allow the Holy Spirit to use
the gift. This is the way it should be, so that we will have
divine utterances only by the Spirit. I would be very sorry
to use a gift in my own strength, but the Giver has all
power to use all nine gifts of the Holy Spirit.

Three Witnesses to the Baptism

I want to take you to the Scriptures to prove my position that tongues are the evidence of the baptism in the
Holy Spirit. Businessmen know that in cases of law
where there are two clear witnesses, they could win a
case before any judge. On the clear evidence of two witnesses, any judge will give a verdict. What has God
given us? He has given us three clear witnesses on the

baptism in the Holy Spirit—more than are necessary in law courts. The first was given on the Day of Pentecost: *"They were all filled with the Holy Spirit and began to speak with other tongues, as the Spirit gave them utterance"* (Acts 2:4). Here we have the original pattern. God gave to Peter an eternal word that couples this experience with the promise that came before it: *"This is what was spoken by the prophet Joel"* (v. 16). God wants you to have this—nothing less than this. He wants you to receive the baptism in the Holy Spirit according to this original Pentecostal pattern.

In Acts 10, we have another witness. Peter was in the house of Cornelius, because Cornelius had had a vision of a holy angel and had sent for Peter. A woman said to me one day, "You don't admit that I am filled and baptized with the Holy Spirit. Why, I was ten days and ten nights on my back before the Lord, and He was flooding my soul with joy." I said, "Praise the Lord, sister, that was only the beginning. The disciples were waiting for that length of time, and the mighty power of God fell upon them. The Bible tells us what happened when the power fell." And that is just what happened in the house of Cornelius. The Holy Spirit fell on all those who heard the Word.

> *And those of the circumcision who believed were astonished, as many as came with Peter, because the gift of the Holy Spirit had been poured out on the Gentiles also.* (Acts 10:45)

What convinced these prejudiced Jews that the Holy Spirit had come? *"For they heard them speak with tongues and magnify God"* (v. 46). There was no other way for them to know. This evidence could not be contradicted. It is the biblical evidence.

Biblical Evidence of the Baptism

We have heard two witnesses, and that is sufficient to satisfy the world. But God goes one better. Let us look at Acts 19:6, which records Paul ministering to certain disciples in Ephesus:

> *And when Paul had laid hands on them, the Holy Spirit came upon them, and they spoke with tongues and prophesied.*

These Ephesians received the identical biblical evidence that the apostles had received at the beginning, and they prophesied in addition. Three times the Scriptures show us this evidence of the baptism in the Spirit. I do not glorify tongues. No, by God's grace, I glorify the Giver of tongues. And above all, I glorify Him whom the Holy Spirit has come to reveal to us, the Lord Jesus Christ. It is He who sends the Holy Spirit, and I glorify Him because He makes no distinction between us and those who believed at the beginning.

But what are tongues for? Look at the second verse of 1 Corinthians 14, and you will see a very blessed truth. Oh, hallelujah! Have you been there, beloved? I tell you, God wants to take you there. *"For he who speaks in a tongue does not speak to men but to God, for no one understands him; however, in the spirit he speaks mysteries."* The passage goes on to say, *"He who speaks in a tongue edifies himself"* (v. 4).

Enter into the promises of God. It is your inheritance. You will do more in one year if you are really filled with the Holy Spirit than you could do in fifty years apart from Him.

13

Concerning Spiritual Gifts

Now concerning spiritual gifts, brethren,
I do not want you to be ignorant.
—1 Corinthians 12:1

There is a great weakness in the church of Christ because of an awful ignorance concerning the Spirit of God and the gifts He has come to bring. God wants us to be powerful in every way because of the revelation of the knowledge of His will concerning the power and manifestation of His Spirit. He desires us to be continually hungry to receive more and more of His Spirit.

In the past, I have organized many conferences, and I have found that it is better to have a man on my platform who has not received the baptism but who is hungry for all that God has for him, than a man who has received the baptism and is satisfied and has settled down and become stationary and stagnant. But of course I would prefer a man who is baptized with the Holy Spirit and is still hungry for more of God. A man who is not hungry to receive more of God is out of order in any Christian conference.

The Importance of Being Filled

It is impossible to overestimate the importance of being filled with the Spirit. It is impossible for us to meet the conditions of the day, to *"walk in the light as He is in the light"* (1 John 1:7), to subdue kingdoms and work righteousness and bind the power of the devil, unless we are filled with the Holy Spirit.

We read that, in the early church, *"they continued steadfastly in the apostles' doctrine and fellowship, in the breaking of bread, and in prayers"* (Acts 2:42). It is important for us also to continue steadfastly in these same things.

For some years I was associated with the Plymouth Brethren. They are very strong in the Word and are sound on water baptism. They do not neglect the communion service; rather, they have it on the morning of every Lord's Day, as the early church did. These people seem to have everything except the match. They have the wood, but they need the fire; then they would be all ablaze.

Because they lack the fire of the Holy Spirit, there is no life in their meetings. One young man who attended their meetings received the baptism with the speaking in other tongues as the Spirit gave utterance (Acts 2:4). The brethren were very upset about this, and they came to the young man's father and said to him, "You must take your son aside and tell him to cease." They did not want any disturbance.

The father told the son, "My boy, I have been attending this church for twenty years and have never seen anything of this kind. We are established in the truth and do not want anything new. We won't have it."

The son replied, "If that is God's plan, I will obey, but somehow or other I don't think it is."

As they were going home, the horse stood still; the wheels of their carriage were in deep ruts. The father pulled at the reins, but the horse did not move. He asked, "What do you think is up?"

The son answered, "It has gotten established." God save us from becoming stationary.

God wants us to understand spiritual gifts and to *"earnestly desire the best gifts"* (1 Cor. 12:31). He also wants us to enter into the *"more excellent way"* (v. 31) of the fruit of the Spirit. We must implore God for these gifts. It is a serious thing to have the baptism and yet be stationary. To live two days in succession on the same spiritual plane is a tragedy. We must be willing to deny ourselves everything to receive the revelation of God's truth and to receive the fullness of the Spirit. Only that will satisfy God, and nothing less must satisfy us.

A young Russian received the Holy Spirit and was mightily clothed with power from on high. Some sisters were anxious to know the secret of his power. The secret of his power was a continuous waiting upon God. As the Holy Spirit filled him, it seemed as though every breath became a prayer, and so his entire ministry was continually increasing.

I knew a man who was full of the Holy Spirit and would preach only when he knew that he was mightily anointed by the power of God. He was once asked to preach at a Methodist church. He was staying at the minister's house and he said, "You go on to church, and I will follow."

The place was packed with people, but this man did not show up. The Methodist minister, becoming anxious, sent his little girl to inquire why he did not come. As she came to the bedroom door, she heard him crying out three times, "I will not go." She went back and reported that she had heard the man say three times that he would not go. The minister was troubled about it, but almost immediately afterward the man came in. As he preached that night, the power of God was tremendously manifested.

The pastor later asked him, "Why did you tell my daughter that you were not coming?"

He answered, "I know when I am filled. I am an ordinary man, and I told the Lord that I did not dare to go and would not go until He gave me a fresh filling of the Spirit. The moment the glory filled me and overflowed, I came to the meeting."

Yes, there is a power, a blessing, an assurance, a rest in the presence of the Holy Spirit. You can feel His presence and know that He is with you. You do not need to spend an hour without this inner knowledge of His holy presence. With His power upon you, there can be no failure. You are above par all the time.

"You know that you were Gentiles, carried away to these dumb idols, however you were led" (1 Cor. 12:2). This is the age of the Gentiles. When the Jews refused the blessings of God, He scattered them, and He has grafted the Gentiles into the olive tree where many of the Jews were broken off. (See Romans 11:17–25.)

There has never been a time when God has been so favorable to a people who were not a people. (See 1 Peter 2:9–10.) He has brought in the Gentiles to carry out His purpose of preaching the Gospel to all nations and receiving the power of the Holy Spirit to accomplish this task. It is because of God's mercy that He has turned to the Gentiles and made us partakers of all the blessings that belong to the Jews. Here, under this canopy of glory, because we believe, we get all the blessings of faithful Abraham.

Guard against Error

Therefore I make known to you that no one speaking by the Spirit of God calls Jesus accursed, and no one can say that Jesus is Lord except by the Holy Spirit. (1 Cor. 12:3)

Many evil, deceiving spirits have been sent forth in these last days who endeavor to rob Jesus of His lordship and of His rightful place. Many people are opening the doors to these latest devils, such as New Theology and New Thought and Christian Science. These evil cults deny the fundamental truths of God's Word. They all deny eternal punishment and the deity of Jesus Christ. You will never see the baptism of the Holy Spirit come upon a man who accepts these errors, nor will you see anyone receive the baptism who puts Mary in the place of the Holy Spirit.

No one can know he is saved by works. If you ever speak to someone who believes this, you will know that he is not definite on the matter of the new birth. He cannot be. And there is another thing: you will never find a Jehovah's Witness baptized in the Holy Spirit. The same is true for a member of any other cult who does not believe that the Lord Jesus Christ is preeminent.

The all-important thing is to make Jesus Lord of your life. *"If you confess with your mouth the Lord Jesus and believe in your heart that God has raised Him from the dead, you will be saved"* (Romans 10:9). *"For to this end Christ died and rose and lived again, that He might be Lord of both the dead and the living"* (Romans 14:9). Men can become lopsided by emphasizing the truth of divine healing. Men can get into error by preaching on water baptism all the time. But we never go wrong in

155

exalting the Lord Jesus Christ, in giving Him the preeminent place and glorifying Him as both Lord and Christ, yes, as "very God of very God." As we are filled with the Holy Spirit, our one desire is to glorify Him. We need to be filled with the Spirit to get the full revelation of the Lord Jesus Christ.

God's command is for us to *"be filled with the Spirit"* (Eph. 5:18). We are no good if we have only a full cup. We need to have an overflowing cup all the time. It is a tragedy not to live in the fullness of overflowing. See that you never live below the overflowing tide.

Use the Gifts Properly

"There are diversities of gifts, but the same Spirit" (1 Cor. 12:4). Every manifestation of the Spirit is given *"for the profit of all"* (v. 7). When the Holy Spirit is moving in an assembly of believers and His gifts are in operation, everyone will profit.

I have seen some people who have been terribly off track. They believe in gifts—prophecy, in particular—and they use these gifts apart from the power of the Holy Spirit. We must look to the Holy Spirit to show us how to use the gifts, what they are for, and when to use them, so that we may never use them without the power of the Holy Spirit. I do not know of anything that is so awful today as people using a gift without the power. Never do it. May God save us from doing it.

While a man who is filled with the Holy Spirit may not be conscious of having any gift of the Spirit, the gifts can be made manifest through him. I have gone to many places to minister, and I have found that, under the unction, or anointing, of the Holy Spirit, many wonderful things have happened in the midst of the assembly when the glory of the Lord was upon the people. Any man who is filled with God and filled with His Spirit might at any moment have any of the nine gifts listed in 1 Corinthians 12 made manifest through him, without knowing that he has a gift.

Sometimes I have wondered whether it is better to always be full of the Holy Spirit and to see signs and wonders and miracles without any consciousness of possessing a gift or whether it is better to know one has a gift. If you have received the gifts of the Spirit and they have been blessed, you should never under any circumstances use them without the power of God upon you pressing the gift through. Some have used the prophetic gift without the holy touch, and they have come into the realm of the natural. It has brought ruin, caused dissatisfaction, broken hearts, and upset assemblies. Do not seek the gifts unless you have purposed to abide in the Holy Spirit. They should be manifested only in the power of the Holy Spirit.

Use the Gifts with Wisdom

The Lord will allow you to be very drunk in the Spirit in His presence, but sober among people. I like to see people so filled with the Spirit that they are drunk in the Spirit like the disciples were on the Day of Pentecost, but I don't like to see people drunk in the Spirit in the wrong place. That is what troubles us: somebody being drunk in the Spirit in a place of worship where a lot of people come in who know nothing about the Word. If you allow yourself to be drunk there, you send people away; they look at you instead of seeing God. They condemn the whole thing because you have not been sober at the right time.

Paul wrote, *"For if we are beside ourselves, it is for God; or if we are of sound mind, it is for you"* (2 Cor. 5:13). You can be beside yourself. You can go a bit further than being drunk; you can dance, if you will do it at the right time. So many things are commendable when all the people are in the Spirit. Many things are very foolish if the people around you are not in the Spirit. We must be careful not to have a good time in the Lord at the expense of somebody else. When you have a good time, you must see that the spiritual conditions in the place lend themselves to it and that the people are falling in line with you. Then you will always find it a blessing.

While it is right to *"earnestly desire the best gifts"* (1 Cor. 12:31), you must recognize that the all-important thing is to be filled with the power of the Holy Spirit Himself. You will never have trouble with people who are filled with the power of the Holy Spirit, but you will have a lot of trouble with people who have the gifts but no power. The Lord does not want us to *"come short in* [any] *gift"* (1 Cor. 1:7). But at the same time, He wants us to be so filled with the Holy Spirit that it will be the Holy Spirit manifesting Himself through the gifts. Where the glory of God alone is desired, you can expect that every gift that is needed will be made manifest. To glorify God is better than to idolize gifts. We prefer the Spirit of God to any gift; but we can see the manifestation of the Trinity in the gifts: different gifts but the same Spirit, different administrations but the same Lord, diversities of operation but the same God working all in all (1 Cor. 12:4–6). Can you conceive of what it will mean for our triune God to be manifesting Himself in His fullness in our assemblies?

Imagine a large locomotive boiler that is being filled with steam. You can see the engine letting off some of the steam as it remains stationary. It looks as though the whole thing might burst. You can see believers who are like that. They start to scream, but that does not edify anyone. However, when the locomotive moves on, it serves the purpose for which it was built and pulls along many cars with goods in them. It is the same way with believers when they are operating in the gifts of the Spirit properly.

Inward Power Manifested Outwardly

It is wonderful to be filled with the power of the Holy Spirit and for Him to serve His own purposes through us. Through our lips, divine utterances flow, our hearts rejoice, and our tongues are glad. It is an inward power that is manifested in outward expression. Jesus Christ is glorified. As your faith in Him is quickened, from within you there *"will flow rivers of living water"* (John 7:38). The Holy Spirit will pour through you like a great river of life, and thousands will be blessed because you are a yielded channel through whom the Spirit may flow.

The most important thing, the one thing that counts, is to see that we are filled with the Holy Spirit, filled to overflowing. Anything less than this is displeasing to God. We are commanded by God to be filled with the Spirit, and in the measure that you lack this, you are that far short of the plan of God. The Lord wants us to move on from *"faith to faith"* (Rom. 1:17), from *"glory to glory"* (2 Cor. 3:18), from fullness to overflowing. It is not good for us to be always thinking in the past tense; rather, we should be moving on to the place where we dare to believe God. He has declared that after the Holy Spirit comes upon us, we will have power (Acts 1:8). I believe there is an avalanche of power from God to be apprehended if we will but catch the vision.

At one time Paul wrote, *"I* [now] *come to visions and revelations"* (2 Cor. 12:1). God has put us in a place where He expects us to have His latest revelation, the revelation of that marvelous fact of *"Christ in* [us]*"* (Col. 1:27) and what this really means. We can understand Christ fully only as we are filled and overflowing with the Spirit of God. Our only safeguard from dropping back into our natural minds, from which we can never get anything, is to be filled and filled again with the Spirit of God, and to be taken on to new visions and revelations. The reason why I emphasize the importance of the fullness of the Holy Spirit is that I want to get you beyond all human plans and thoughts and into the fullness of vision, into the full revelation of the Lord Jesus Christ.

Do you want rest? It is in Jesus. Do you want to be saved from everything the devil is bringing up in these last times? Receive and continue in the fullness of the Holy Spirit, and He will be always revealing to you that all you need for all times is in Christ Jesus your Lord.

I desire to emphasize the importance of the Spirit's ministry and of the manifestation of the Spirit that is *"given to each one for the profit of all"* (1 Cor. 12:7). As you yield to the Spirit of the Lord, He has power over your intellect, over your heart, and over your voice. The Holy Spirit has power to unveil Christ and to project the vision of Christ upon the canvas of your mind. Then He uses your tongue to glorify and magnify Him in a way that you could never do apart from the Spirit's power.

Never say that when you are filled with the Holy Spirit, you are "obligated" to do this or that. When people say that they are obligated to do a particular thing, I know it is not the Spirit of God, but their own spirits, moving them to do what is unseemly and unprofitable. For example, many people spoil prayer meetings by screaming during them. If you want to do that kind of thing, you had better do it down in some cellar, because it does not edify people. I believe that, when the Spirit of God is upon you and moving you to speak as He gives utterance, it will always edify people.

Don't spoil the prayer meeting by continuing to pray when you ought to have stopped. Who spoils a prayer meeting? The person who starts in the Spirit and finishes in the flesh. Nothing is more lovely than prayer, but a prayer meeting is killed if you go on and on in your own spirit after the Spirit of God has finished speaking through you. We say, as we come from some meetings, "That would have been a lovely message, if the preacher had only stopped half an hour before he did." Learn to cease immediately when the anointing of the Spirit lifts. The Holy Spirit is jealous. Your body is the temple of God (1 Cor. 3:16), the office of the Holy Spirit. He does not fill the temple for human glorification, but only for the glory of God. You have no license to continue beyond a "Thus says the Lord."

There is another side to this. God wants the assembly to be as free as possible, and you must not hinder the working of the Spirit, or it will surely bring trouble. You must be prepared to allow a certain amount of extravagance in young and newly baptized souls. You must remember that when you were brought into this life of the Spirit, you had as many extravagances as anybody, but you have now become somewhat "sobered up." It is a pity that some people do get sobered up, for they are not where they were in the early days. We have to look to God for wisdom, so that we do not interfere with or dampen the Spirit, or quench the power of God when He is manifested in our meetings. If you want to have an assembly that is full of life, you must have an assembly that is full of manifestation. Nobody will come to the meetings if there is no manifestation. We need to look to God for special grace, so that we do not move back to looking at things from a natural viewpoint.

If a preacher has lost his anointing, he should inwardly repent, get right with God, and receive the anointing again. We are no good without the anointing of the Spirit of God. If you are filled with the grace of God, you will not judge everybody in the assembly, but you will rather trust everybody; you will not be frightened at what is being done, but you will have a heart to *"believe all things"* (see 1 Corinthians 13:7) and to believe that though there may be some extravagances, the Spirit of God will take control and will see that the Lord Jesus Christ Himself is exalted, glorified, and revealed to hungry hearts who desire to know Him. The Lord wants us to be *"wise in what is good, and simple concerning evil"* (Rom. 16:19). He wants us to be free from distrust, entering into a divine likeness to Jesus that dares to believe that God Almighty will surely watch over all. Hallelujah!

The Holy Spirit is the One who glorifies the Lord Jesus Christ, the One who illuminates Him. If you are filled with the Holy Spirit, it is impossible for you to keep your tongue still. There is no such thing as a mute baptized soul! It is not to be found in the Scriptures or outside of the Scriptures. We are filled with the Spirit in order that we may magnify the Lord, and there should be no meeting in which believers do not glorify, magnify, praise, and worship the Lord in Spirit and in truth (John 4:23–24).

I would like to give a word of caution, for failure often comes through our not recognizing the fact that we are always in the body. We will need our bodies as long as we live, but our bodies are to be used and controlled by the Spirit of God. We are to present our bodies *"holy, acceptable to God, which is* [our] *reasonable service"* (Rom. 12:1). Every member of our bodies must be so sanctified that it works in harmony with the Spirit of God. Our very eyes must be sanctified. God hates the "winking of the eye." From the day that I read in Proverbs what God has to say about the winking of the eye (see Proverbs 6:13; 10:10), I have never winked. I desire that my eyes may be so sanctified that they can always be used for the Lord. The Spirit of God will bring in us a compassion for souls that will be seen in our very eyes.

God has never changed the order of things: first comes the natural, and then comes the spiritual. For instance, when it is on your heart to pray, you begin in the natural, but your second word will probably be under the power of the Spirit. You begin, and then God will take over to the end. It is the same in giving forth utterances under the Spirit's power. You feel the moving of the Spirit within, and you begin to speak in the natural, and then the Spirit of God gives forth utterances. Thousands have missed wonderful blessings because they have not had the faith to move out and begin in the natural, in faith that the Lord would take them into the realm of the supernatural.

When you receive the Holy Spirit, you receive God's gift, in whom are all the gifts of the Spirit. Paul counseled Timothy to *"stir up the gift"* (2 Tim. 1:6) that was within him. You have power to stir up God's gift within you. The way you stir up the gift within you is by beginning in faith. Then He gives forth what is needed for the occasion. You would never begin unless you were full of God. When we yield to timidity and fear, we simply yield to the devil. Satan whispers, "It is all self." He is a liar. I have learned that if the Spirit of God is stirring me up, I have no hesitation in beginning to speak in tongues, and the Spirit of God gives me utterance and gives me the interpretation. I find that every time I yield to the Lord in this way, I get a divine touch. I receive guidance or direction from the Spirit of God, and the meeting is taken to a higher plane because faith was exercised.

Suppose you attend a meeting in faith, believing that the Lord is going to meet you there. But suppose also that the evangelist is not in harmony with God, and the people in the assembly are not getting what God wants. The Lord knows it. He knows His people are hungry. What happens? He will take perhaps the smallest vessels and put His power upon them. As they yield to the Spirit, they break forth in tongues. Another yields to the Spirit, and the interpretation is given. The Lord's church has to be fed, and the Lord will use this means of speaking to His people. Pentecostal people cannot be satisfied with a natural message. They are in touch with heavenly things and cannot be satisfied with anything less. They feel when there is something lacking in a meeting, they look to God, and He supplies what is lacking.

When a person is filled with the Spirit, he has no conception of what he has. We are so limited in our conception of what we have received. The only way we can know the power that has been given to us is through the ministry and manifestation of the Spirit of God. Do you think that Peter and John knew what they had when they went up to the temple to pray? (See Acts 3:1–10.) They were limited in thought and limited in their expression of thought. The nearer we get to God, the more conscious we are of the poverty of human beings, and we cry out with Isaiah, *"I am undone;...I am a man of unclean lips"* (Isa. 6:5). But the Lord will bring the precious blood and the flaming coals (see verses 6–7) for cleansing and refining, and will send us out to labor for Him empowered by His Spirit.

God has sent forth this outpouring so that we may all be brought into a revelation of our sonship—that we have *"become sons of God"* (John 1:12 KJV), that we are to be like the Lord Jesus Christ, that we are to have the powers of sonship, the power to lay hold of what is weak and to quicken it. The baptism of the Spirit is for the purpose of making us sons of God with power. (See Romans 1:4.) We will be conscious of our human limitations, but we will not limit the Holy One who has come to dwell within us. We must believe that since the Holy Spirit has come upon us, we are indeed sons of God with power. Never say "I can't." *"All things are possible to him who believes"* (Mark 9:23). Launch out into the deep and believe that God has His all for you and that you can do all things through Him who strengthens you (Phil 4:13).

Peter and John knew that they had been in the Upper Room, that they had felt the glory and had been given divine utterances. They had seen conviction on the faces of the people. They knew that they had come into a wonderful thing. They knew that what they had would be continuously increasing, and that it would always be necessary to cry, "Enlarge the vessel, so that the Holy Spirit may have more room within." They knew that all the old things had been moved away, that they had entered into an increasing and ever increasing knowledge of God, that it was their Master's wish that they be filled with the Spirit of God and with power every day and every hour. The secret of power is the unveiling of Christ, the all-powerful One within, the Revelation of God who comes to abide within us.

As Peter and John looked upon the crippled man at the Beautiful Gate of the temple, they were filled with compassion. They were prompted by the Spirit to stop and speak with him. They said to the lame man, *"Look at us"* (Acts 3:4). It was God's plan that the man should open his eyes with expectation. Peter said, "Of silver and gold we have none. But we have something else, and we will give it to you. We don't know what it is, but we give it to you. It is all in the name of Jesus." (See verse 6.) And then the ministry of God began. You begin in faith, and you see what will happen. It is hidden from us at the beginning, but as we have faith in God, He will come forth. The coming forth of the power is not of us but of God. There is no limit to what He will do. It is all in a nutshell as you believe God. That's why, when Peter said, *"What I do have I give you: In the name of Jesus Christ of Nazareth, rise up and walk"* (v. 6), the man who had been lame for forty years stood up and began to leap and entered into the temple *"walking, leaping, and praising God"* (v. 8).

"For to one is given the word of wisdom through the Spirit" (1 Cor. 12:8). I want you to keep in mind the importance of never expecting the gifts of the Spirit apart from the power of the Spirit. In earnestly desiring the best gifts (v. 31), earnestly desire to be so full of God and His glory that the gifts in manifestation will always glorify Him. We do not know all and we cannot know all that can be brought forth in the manifestation of the word of wisdom. One word of wisdom from God, one flash of light on the Word of God, is sufficient to save us from a thousand pitfalls. People have built without a word from God, they have bought things without a word from God, and they have been ensnared. They have lacked that word of wisdom that will bring them into God's plan for

their lives. I have been in many places where I have needed a word of wisdom from God and it has been granted to me.

I will give you one instance. There is one thing I am very grateful to the Lord for, and that is that He has given me grace not to have a desire for money. The love of money is a great hindrance to many; many a man is crippled in his ministry because he lets his heart run after financial matters. I was out walking one day when I met a godly man who lived opposite me, and he said, "My wife and I have been talking together about selling our house, and we feel constrained to sell it to you." As we talked together, he persuaded me to buy his place, and before we said good-bye, I told him that I would take it. We always make big mistakes when we are in a hurry.

I told my wife what I had promised, and she said, "How will you manage it?" I told her that I had managed things so far, but I did not know how I was going to get through this. I somehow knew that I was out of the divine order. Still, when a fellow gets out of the divine order, it seems that the last person he goes to is God. I was relying on an architect to help me with the finances, but that scheme fell through. Then I turned to my relatives, and I was certainly sweating as one after another turned me down. I tried my friends and managed no better.

My wife said to me, "You have not been to God yet." What could I do?

I have a certain place in our house where I go to pray. I have been there very often. As I went there, I said, "Lord, if You will get me out of this scrape, I will never trouble You about this kind of thing again." As I waited on the Lord, He gave me just one word. It seemed like a ridiculous thing, but it was the wisest counsel. There is divine wisdom in every word He speaks.

I came down to my wife saying, "What do you think? The Lord has told me to go to Brother Webster. It seems very ridiculous, for he is one of the poorest men I know." He was the poorest man I knew, but he was also the richest man I knew, for he knew God.

My wife said, "Do what God says, and it will be right."

I went off at once to see him, and he said as he greeted me, "Smith, what brings you here so early?"

I answered, "The word of God." Then I said to him, "About three weeks ago, I promised to buy a man's house, but I am short five hundred dollars. I have tried to get this money, but somehow I seem to have missed God."

"How is it," he asked, "that you have come to me only now?"

I answered, "Because I went to the Lord about it only last night."

"Well," he said, "it is a strange thing. Three weeks ago, I had five hundred dollars. For years I have been putting money into a cooperative, and three weeks ago I had to go and draw out five hundred dollars. I hid it under the mattress. Come with me, and you shall have it. Take it. I hope it will bring as great a blessing to you as it has been a trouble to me."

I had had a word from God, and all my troubles were ended. This has been multiplied in a hundred ways since that time. If I had been walking along filled with the Holy Spirit, I would not have bought that house and would not have had all that strain. I believe the Lord wants to loose us from the things of earth. But I am ever grateful for that word from God.

There have been times in my life when I have been in great crises and under great weight of intercession. I have gone to a meeting without knowing what I would say, but somehow or other God would grant the coming forth of some word of wisdom under the power of the Spirit, just what some souls in that meeting needed. As we look to God, His mind will be made known, and His revelation and His word of wisdom will be forthcoming.

14

The Word of Knowledge and the Gift of Faith

To another [is given] *the word of knowledge through the same Spirit, to another faith by the same Spirit.*
—1 Corinthians 12:8–9

We have not passed this way before. I believe that the devil has many devices and that they are worse today than ever before. But I also believe that there is to be a full manifestation on the earth of the power and glory of God to defeat every device of the enemy.

In Ephesians we are told:

> *Endeavor...to keep the unity of the Spirit in the bond of peace. There is one body and one Spirit...one Lord, one faith, one baptism; one God and Father of all, who is above all and through all, and in you all.* (Eph. 4:3–6)

The baptism of the Spirit is to make us all one. Paul told us that *"by one Spirit we were all baptized into one body...and have all been made to drink into one Spirit"*

171

(1 Cor. 12:13). It is God's intention that we speak the same thing. If we all have the full revelation of the Spirit of God, we will all see the same thing. Paul asked the Corinthians, *"Is Christ divided?"* (1 Cor. 1:13). When the Holy Spirit has full control, Christ is never divided. His body is not divided; there is no division. Schism and division are products of the carnal mind.

The Word of Knowledge

How important it is that we have the manifestation of *"the word of knowledge"* in our midst. The same Spirit who brings forth the word of wisdom brings forth the word of knowledge. The revelation of the mysteries of God comes by the Spirit, and we must have a supernatural word of knowledge in order to convey to others the things that the Spirit of God has revealed. The Spirit of God reveals Christ in all His wonderful fullness, and He shows Him to us from the beginning to the end of the Scriptures. It is the Word that make us *"wise for salvation"* (2 Tim. 3:15) and that open to us the depths of the kingdom of heaven, revealing all of the divine mind to us.

There are thousands of people who read and study the Word of God, but it is not quickened to them. The Bible is a dead letter except by the Spirit. The Word of God can never be vital and powerful in us except by the Spirit. The words that Christ spoke were not just dead words, but they were spirit and life (John 6:63). And so, it is the intention of God that a living word, a word of truth, the word of God, a supernatural word of knowledge will come forth from us through the power of the Spirit of God. It is the Holy Spirit who will bring forth utterances from our lips and a divine revelation of all the mind of God.

The child of God ought to thirst for the Word. He should know nothing else but the Word, and he should know nothing among men except Jesus (1 Cor. 2:2). *"Man shall not live by bread alone, but by every word that proceeds from the mouth of God"* (Matt. 4:4). It is as we feed on the Word and meditate on the message it contains that the Spirit of God can vitalize what we have received and bring forth through us the word of knowledge. This word will be as full of power and life as when He, the Spirit of God, moved upon holy men in ancient times and gave them the inspired Scriptures. All the Scriptures were inspired by God (2 Tim. 3:16) as they came forth at the beginning, and through the same Spirit they should come forth from us vitalized, *"living and powerful, and sharper than any two-edged sword"* (Heb. 4:12).

With the gifts of the Spirit should come the fruit of the Spirit. With wisdom we should have love, with knowledge we should have joy, and with faith we should have the fruit of peace. Faith is always accompanied by peace. Faith always rests. Faith laughs at impossibilities. Salvation is by faith, through grace, and *"it is the gift of God"* (Eph. 2:8).

The Power of Faith

We are kept by the power of God through faith. God gives faith, and nothing can take it away. By faith we have power to enter into the wonderful things of God. There are three kinds of faith: saving faith, which is the gift of God; the faith of the Lord Jesus; and the gift of faith. You will remember the word that the Lord Jesus Christ gave to Paul, to which he referred in Acts 26, where the Lord commissioned him to go to the Gentiles:

EVER INCREASING FAITH

To open their eyes, in order to turn them from
darkness to light, and from the power of Satan to
God, that they may receive forgiveness of sins
*and an inheritance among those **who are sanc-***
tified by faith in Me.

(Acts 26:18, emphasis added)

Oh, this wonderful faith of the Lord Jesus. Our faith comes to an end. Many times I have been to the place where I have had to tell the Lord, "I have used all the faith I have," and then He has placed His own faith within me.

One of my fellow workers in ministry said to me at Christmastime, "Wigglesworth, I was never so near the end of my finances in my life." I replied, "Thank God, you are just at the opening of God's treasures." It is when we are at the end of our own resources that we can enter into the riches of God's resources. It is when we possess nothing that we can possess all things. The Lord will always meet you when you have a living faith.

I was in Ireland one time, and I went to a house and said to the lady who came to the door, "Is Brother Wallace here?" She replied, "Oh, he has gone to Bangor, but God has sent you here for me. I need you. Come in." She told me her husband was a deacon of the Presbyterian Church. She herself had received the baptism of the Spirit while she was a member of the Presbyterian Church, but they did not accept it as from God. The people of the church said to her husband, "This thing cannot go on. We don't want you to be a deacon any longer, and your wife is not wanted in the church."

The man was very enraged, and he became incensed against his wife. It seemed as though an evil spirit had possessed him, and the home that had once been peaceful became very terrible. Finally, he left home without leaving behind any money for his wife. The woman asked me what she should do.

We went to prayer, and before we had prayed five minutes, the woman was mightily filled with the Holy Spirit. I said to her, "Sit down and let me talk to you. Are you often in the Spirit like this?"

She said, "Yes, and what could I do without the Holy Spirit now?"

I said to her, "The situation is yours. The Word of God says that you have power to sanctify your husband. (See 1 Corinthians 7:14.) Dare to believe the Word of God. Now the first thing we must do is to pray that your husband comes back tonight."

She said, "I know he won't."

I replied, "If we agree together, it is done."

She said, "I will agree."

Then I said to her, "When he comes home, show him all possible love; lavish everything upon him. If he won't hear what you have to say, let him go to bed. The situation is yours. Get down before God and claim him for the Lord. Get into the glory just as you have gotten into it today, and as the Spirit of God prays through you, you will find that God will grant all the desires of your heart."

A month later I saw this sister at a conference. She told how her husband came home that night. He went to bed, but she prayed right through to victory and then placed her hands on him. The moment she laid her hands on him, he cried out for mercy. The Lord saved him and baptized him in the Holy Spirit. The power of God is beyond all our conception. The trouble is that we do not have the power of God in a full manifestation because of our finite thoughts, but as we go on and let God have His way, there is no limit to what our limitless God will do in response to a limitless faith. But you will never get anywhere unless you are in constant pursuit of all the power of God.

One day when I came home from our open-air meeting at eleven o'clock, I found that my wife was out. I asked, "Where is she?" I was told that she was down at Mitchell's. I had seen Mitchell that day and knew that he was at the point of death. I knew that it would be impossible for him to survive the day unless the Lord undertook to heal him.

There are many who let up in sickness and do not take hold of the life of the Lord Jesus Christ that is provided for them. For example, I was taken to see a woman who was dying, and I said to her, "How are things with you?"

She answered, "I have faith; I believe."

I said, "You know that you do not have faith. You know that you are dying. It is not faith that you have; it is language." There is a difference between language and faith. I saw that she was in the hands of the devil. There was no possibility of life until he was removed from the premises. I hate the devil, and I laid hold of the woman and shouted, "Come out, you demon of death. I command you to come out in the name of Jesus." In one minute she stood on her feet in victory.

But to return to the case of Brother Mitchell, I hurried down to the house, and as I got near, I heard terrible screams. I knew that something had happened. I saw Mrs. Mitchell on the staircase and asked, "What's up?"

She replied, "He is gone! He is gone!"

I just passed by her and went into the room. Immediately I saw that Mitchell had gone. I could not understand it, but I began to pray. My wife was always afraid that I would go too far, and she laid hold of me and said, "Don't, Dad! Don't you see that he is dead?" I continued to pray and my wife continued to cry out to me, "Don't, Dad. Don't you see that he is dead?" But I continued praying.

I got as far as I could with my own faith, and then God laid hold of me. Oh, it was such a laying hold that I could believe for anything. The faith of the Lord Jesus laid hold of me, and a solid peace came into my heart. I shouted, "He lives! He lives! He lives!" And he is living today.

There is a difference between our faith and the faith of the Lord Jesus. The faith of the Lord Jesus is needed. We must change faith from time to time. Your faith may get to a place where it wavers. The faith of Christ never wavers. When you have His faith, the thing is finished. When you have that faith, you will never look at things as they are. You will see the things of nature give way to the things of the Spirit; you will see the temporal swallowed up in the eternal.

I was at a camp meeting in Cazadero, California, several years ago, and a remarkable thing happened. A man came who was stone deaf. I prayed for him, and I knew that God had healed him. Then came the test. He would always move his chair up to the platform, and every time I got up to speak, he would get up as close as he could and strain his ears to catch what I had to say.

The devil said, "It isn't done."

I declared, "It is done."

This went on for three weeks, and then the manifestation came. He could hear distinctly from sixty yards away. When his ears were opened, he thought it was so great that he had to stop the meeting and tell everybody about it. I met him in Oakland recently, and he was hearing perfectly. As we remain steadfast and unmovable on the ground of faith, we will see in perfect manifestation what we are believing for.

The Gift of Faith

People say to me, "Don't you have the gift of faith?" I say that it is an important gift, but that what is still more important is for us to be making an advancement in God every moment. Looking at the Word of God, I find that its realities are greater to me today than they were yesterday. It is the most sublime, joyful truth that God brings an enlargement, always an enlargement. There is nothing dead, dry, or barren in this life of the Spirit; God is always moving us on to something higher, and as we move on in the Spirit, our faith will always rise to the occasion as different circumstances arise.

This is how the gift of faith is manifested. You see something, and you know that your own faith is nothing in the situation. The other day I was in San Francisco. I was sitting on a streetcar, and I saw a boy in great agony on the street. I said, "Let me get out." I rushed to where the boy was. He was in agony because of stomach cramps. I put my hands on his stomach in the name of Jesus. The boy jumped and stared at me with astonishment. He found himself instantly free of pain. The gift of faith dared in the face of everything. It is as we are in the Spirit that the Spirit of God will operate this gift anywhere and at any time.

When the Spirit of God is operating this gift within a person, He causes him to know what God is going to do. When the man with the withered hand was in the synagogue, Jesus got all the people to look to see what would happen. The gift of faith always knows the results. Jesus said to the man, *"Stretch out your hand"* (Matt. 12:13). His word had creative force. He was not speculating. He spoke and something happened. He spoke at the beginning, and the world came into being. He speaks today, and things such as I have just described have to come to pass. He is the Son of God, and He came to bring us into sonship. He was the *"firstfruits"* of the Resurrection (1 Cor. 15:20), and He calls us to be *"firstfruits"* (James 1:18), to be the same kind of fruit as Himself.

There is an important point here. You cannot have the gifts by mere human desire. The Spirit of God distributes them *"to each one individually as He wills"* (1 Cor. 12:11). God cannot trust some people with a gift, but those who have a humble, broken, contrite heart He can trust (Isa. 66:2).

One day I was in a meeting where there were many doctors and eminent men and ministers. It was at a conference, and the power of God fell on the meeting. One humble little girl who served as a waitress opened her being to the Lord, and she was immediately filled with the Holy Spirit and began to speak in tongues. All these big men stretched their necks and looked up to see what was happening. They were saying, "Who is it?" Then they learned it was "the servant." Nobody received except the servant! These things are hidden and kept back from the *"wise and prudent"* (Matt. 11:25), but the little children, the humble ones, are the ones who receive. We cannot have faith if we show undue deference to one another. A man who is going on with God won't accept honor from his fellow beings. God honors the man who has a broken, contrite spirit. How can I get to that place?

So many people want to do great things and to be seen doing them, but the one whom God will use is the one who is willing to be hidden. My Lord Jesus never said He could do things, but He did them. When that funeral procession was coming up from Nain with the widow's son being carried in an open coffin, Jesus made them lay the coffin down. (See Luke 7:11–14.) He spoke the word, *"Arise"* (v. 14), and gave the son back to the widow. He had compassion for her. And you and I will never do anything except along the lines of compassion. We will never be able to remove the cancer until we are immersed so deeply in the power of the Holy Spirit that the compassion of Christ is moving through us.

I find that in everything my Lord did, He said that He did not do it but that Another who was in Him did the work (John 14:10). What a holy submission! He was just an instrument for the glory of God. Have we reached a place where we dare to be trusted with the gift? I see in 1 Corinthians 13 that if I have faith to move mountains and do not have love, all is a failure. When my love is so deepened in God that I move only for the glory of God, that I seek only the glory of God, then the gifts can be made manifest. God wants to be manifested and to manifest His glory to those who are humble.

A faint heart can never have a gift. Two things are essential: first, love; and second, determination—a boldness of faith that will cause God to fulfill His Word.

When I was baptized in the Holy Spirit, I had a wonderful time and had utterances in the Spirit, but for some time afterward, I did not again speak in tongues. One day, as I was ministering to another, the Lord again gave me utterances in the Spirit. After this, I was going down the road one day and speaking in tongues a long while. There were some gardeners doing their work, and they stuck their heads out over the hedges to see what was going on. I said, "Lord, You have something new for me. You said that when a man speaks in tongues, he should ask for the interpretation. I ask for the interpretation, and I'll stay right here until I get it." And from that hour, the Lord has given me interpretation.

One time I was in Lincolnshire, in England, and came in touch with the old rector of an Episcopal church. He became very interested in what I had to say, and he asked me into his library. I never heard anything sweeter than the prayer the old man uttered as he got down to pray. He began to pray, "Lord, make me holy. Lord, sanctify me."

I called out, "Wake up! Wake up now! Get up and sit in your chair." He sat up and looked at me.

I said to him, "I thought you were holy."

He answered, "Yes."

"Then what makes you ask God to do what He has already done for you?"

He began to laugh and then to speak in tongues. Let us move into the realm of faith and live in the realm of faith and let God have His way.

15

Gifts of Healing and the Working of Miracles

To another [are given] the gifts of healing by the same Spirit; to another the working of miracles.
—1 Corinthians 12:9–10 KJV

G od has given us much in these last days, and where much is given, much will be required (Luke 12:48). The Lord has said to us:

You are the salt of the earth; but if the salt loses its flavor, how shall it be seasoned? It is then good for nothing but to be thrown out and trampled underfoot by men. (Matt. 5:13)

Our Lord Jesus expressed a similar thought when He said, *"If anyone does not abide in Me, he is cast out as a branch and is withered; and they gather them and throw them into the fire, and they are burned"* (John 15:6). On the other hand, He told us, *"If you abide in Me, and My words abide in you, you will ask what you desire, and it shall be done for you"* (John 15:7).

If we do not move on with the Lord in these days, and if we do not walk in the light of revealed truth, we will become as flavorless salt or a withered branch. This one thing we must do: *"Forgetting those things which are behind"*—both the past failures and the past blessings— we must reach forth for those things that are before us and *"press toward the mark for the prize of the high calling of God in Christ Jesus"* (Phil. 3:13–14 KJV).

For many years, the Lord has been moving me on and keeping me from spiritual stagnation. When I was in the Wesleyan Methodist Church, I was sure I was saved, and I was sure I was all right. The Lord said to me, "Come out," and I came out. When I was with the people known as the Brethren, I was sure I was all right then. But the Lord said, "Come out." Then I went into the Salvation Army. At that time, it was full of life, and there were revivals everywhere. But the Salvation Army went into natural things, and the great revivals that they had in those early days ceased. The Lord said to me, "Come out," and I came out. I have had to come out three times since.

I believe that this Pentecostal revival that we are now in is the best thing that the Lord has on the earth today; and yet I believe that God will bring something out of this revival that is going to be still better. God has no use for anyone who is not hungering and thirsting for even more of Himself and His righteousness.

The Lord has told us to *"earnestly desire the best gifts"* (1 Cor. 12:31), and we need to earnestly desire those gifts that will bring Him the most glory. We need to see the gifts of healing and the working of miracles in operation today. Some say it is necessary for us to have the gift of discernment in operation with the gifts of healing, but even apart from this gift, I believe that the

Holy Spirit will have a divine revelation for us as we deal with the sick.

Most people think they have discernment; but if they would turn their discernment on themselves for twelve months, they would never want to "discern" again. The gift of discernment is not criticism. I am satisfied that in Pentecostal circles today, our paramount need is more perfect love.

Perfect love will never want the preeminence in everything; it will never want to take the place of another; it will always be willing to take the back seat. If you go to a Bible conference, there is always someone who wants to give a message, who wants to be heard. If you have a desire to go to a conference, you should have three things settled in your mind: Do I want to be heard? Do I want to be seen? Do I want anything on the line of finances? If I have these things in my heart, I have no right to be there.

The one thing that must move us is the constraining love of God to minister for Him. A preacher always loses out when he gets his mind on finances. It is advisable for Pentecostal preachers to avoid making much of finances except to stir people up to help support our missionaries financially. A preacher who gets big collections for the missionaries never needs to fear; the Lord will take care of his finances.

A preacher should not arrive at a place and say that God has sent him. I am always fearful when I hear a man advertising this. If he is sent by God, the believers will know it. God has His plans for His servants, and we must live in His plans so completely that He will place us where He wants us. If you seek nothing but the will of God, He will always put you in the right place at the right time.

I want you to see that the gifts of healing and the working of miracles are part of the Spirit's plan and will come forth in operation as we are working along that plan. I must know the movement of the Spirit and the voice of God. I must understand the will of God if I am to see the gifts of the Spirit in operation.

Ministering Healing

The gifts of healing are so varied. You may go to see ten people, and every case will be different. I am never happier in the Lord than when I am in a bedroom with a sick person. I have had more revelations of the Lord's presence when I have ministered to the sick at their bedsides than at any other time. It is as your heart goes out to the needy ones in deep compassion that the Lord manifests His presence. You are able to discern their conditions. It is then that you know you must be filled with the Spirit to deal with the conditions before you.

When people are sick, you frequently find that they are ignorant about Scripture. They usually know three Scriptures, though. They know about Paul's *"thorn in the flesh"* (2 Cor. 12:7); they know that Paul told Timothy to take *"a little wine"* for his *"stomach's sake"* (1 Tim. 5:23); and they know that Paul left someone sick somewhere, but they don't remember his name or the place, and they don't know in what chapter of the Bible it is found. (See 2 Timothy 4:20.) Most people think they have a thorn in the flesh. The chief thing in dealing with a person who is sick is to discern his exact condition. As you are ministering under the Spirit's power, the Lord will let you see just what will be the most helpful and the most faith-inspiring to him.

186

When I was in the plumbing business, I enjoyed praying for the sick. Urgent calls would come, and I would have no time to wash. With my hands all black, I would preach to these sick ones, my heart all aglow with love. Ah, your heart must be in it when you pray for the sick. You have to get right to the bottom of the cancer with a divine compassion, and then you will see the gifts of the Spirit in operation.

I was called at ten o'clock one night to pray for a young person who was dying of consumption and whom the doctor had given up for dead. As I looked, I saw that unless God intervened, it would be impossible for her to live.

I turned to the mother and said, "Well, Mother, you will have to go to bed."

She said, "Oh, I have not had my clothes off for three weeks."

I said to the daughters, "You will have to go to bed," but they did not want to go. It was the same with the son.

I put on my overcoat and said, "Good-bye, I'm leaving."

They said, "Oh, don't leave us."

I said, "I can do nothing here."

They said, "Oh, if you will stay, we will all go to bed."

I knew that God would not move in an atmosphere of mere natural sympathy and unbelief. They all went to bed, and I stayed, and that was surely a time as I knelt by that bed face-to-face with death and the devil. But God can change the hardest situation and make you know that He is almighty.

Then the fight came. It seemed as though the heavens were brass. I prayed from 11:00 P.M. to 3:30 A.M. I saw the glimmering light on the face of the sufferer and saw her pass away. Satan said, "Now you are done for. You have come from Bradford, and the girl has died on your hands."

I said, "It can't be. God did not send me here for nothing. This is a time to change strength." I remembered the passage that said, *"Men always ought to pray and not lose heart"* (Luke 18:1). Death had taken place, but I knew that God was all-powerful and that He who had split the Red Sea is just the same today. It was a time when I would not accept "No" and God said "Yes."

I looked at the window, and at that moment, the face of Jesus appeared. It seemed as though a million rays of light were coming from His face. As He looked at the one who had just passed away, the color came back to her face. She rolled over and fell asleep. Then I had a glorious time. In the morning she woke early, put on a dressing gown, and walked to the piano. She started to play and to sing a wonderful song. The mother and the sister and the brother all came down to listen. The Lord had intervened. A miracle had been worked.

The Lord is calling us along this way. I thank God for difficult cases. The Lord has called us into heart union with Himself; He wants His bride to have one heart and one Spirit with Him and to do what He Himself loved to do. That case had to be a miracle. The lungs were gone; they were just in shreds. Yet the Lord restored her lungs, making them perfectly sound.

A fruit of the Spirit that must accompany the gift of healing is long-suffering. The man who is persevering with God to be used in healing must be a man of long-suffering. He must always be ready with a word of comfort. If the sick one is in distress and helpless and does not see everything eye-to-eye with you, you must bear with him. Our Lord Jesus Christ was filled with compassion and lived and moved in a place of long-suffering, and we will have to get into this place if we are to help needy ones.

There are times when you pray for the sick, and you seem to be rough with them. But you are not dealing with a person; you are dealing with satanic forces that are binding the person. Your heart is full of love and compassion toward all; however, you are moved to a holy anger as you see the place the devil has taken in the body of the sick one, and you deal with his position with a real forcefulness.

One day a pet dog followed a lady out of her house and ran all around her feet. She said to the dog, "My dear, I cannot have you with me today." The dog wagged its tail and made a big fuss. She said, "Go home, my dear." But the dog did not go. At last she shouted roughly, "Go home," and off it went. Some people deal with the devil like that. Satan can stand all the comfort you like to give him. Cast him out! You are not dealing with the person; you are dealing with the devil. Demon power must be dislodged in the name of the Lord.

You are always right when you dare to deal with sickness as with the devil. Much sickness is caused by some misconduct; there is something wrong, there is some neglect somewhere, and the enemy has had a chance to get in. It is necessary to repent and confess where you have given place to the devil (Eph. 4:27), and then he can be dealt with.

When you deal with a cancer case, recognize that a living evil spirit is destroying the body. I had to pray for a woman in Los Angeles one time who was suffering with a cancerous growth, and as soon as the cancer was cursed, it stopped bleeding. It was dead. The next thing that happened was that the natural body pushed it out, because the natural body had no room for dead matter. It came out like a great big ball with tens of thousands of fibers. All these fibers had been pressing into the flesh. These evil powers move to get further hold of the body's system, but the moment they are destroyed, their hold is gone. Jesus told His disciples that He gave them power to loose and power to bind (Matt. 16:19). It is our privilege in the power of the Holy Spirit to loose the prisoners of the enemy and to let the oppressed go free.

Take your position from the first epistle of John and declare, *"He who is in* [me] *is greater than he who is in the world"* (1 John 4:4). Then recognize that it is not you who has to deal with the power of the devil, but the Greater One who is within you. Oh, what it means to be filled with Him! You can do nothing in yourself, but He who is in you will win the victory. Your being has become the temple of the Holy Spirit. Your mouth, your mind, your whole being may be used and worked upon by the Spirit of God.

I was called to a certain town in Norway. The hall seated about fifteen hundred people. When I got to the place, it was packed, and hundreds were trying to get in. There were some policemen there. The first thing I did was to preach to the people outside the building. Then I said to the policemen, "It hurts me very much that there are more people outside than inside, and I feel I must preach to the people. I would like you to get me the marketplace to preach in." They secured a large park for me, and a big stand was erected, and I was able to preach to thousands.

After the preaching, we had some marvelous cases of healing. One man came a hundred miles, bringing his food with him. He had not been passing anything through his stomach for over a month because he had a large cancer on his stomach. He was healed at that meeting, and opening his package, he began eating for all the people to see.

There was a young woman there with a stiff hand. When she was a child, her mother, instead of making her use her arm, had allowed her to keep it dormant until it was stiff. This young woman was like the woman in the Bible who was bent over with the spirit of infirmity (Luke 13:11). As she stood before me, I cursed the spirit of infirmity in the name of Jesus. It was instantly cast out, and the arm was free. Then she waved her hand all around.

At the close of the meeting, the devil threw two people to the ground with fits. When the devil is manifesting himself, then is the time to deal with him. Both of these people were delivered, and when they stood up and thanked and praised the Lord, what a wonderful time we had.

We need to wake up and strive to believe God. Before God could bring me to this place, He broke me a thousand times. I have wept; I have groaned. I have travailed many a night until God broke me. It seems to me that until God has mowed you down, you can never have this long-suffering, this endurance, for others. We will never have the gifts of healing and the working of miracles in operation unless we stand in the divine power that God gives us, unless we stand believing God and *"having done all"* (Eph. 6:13), we still stand believing.

We have been seeing wonderful miracles during these last days, and they are only a little of what we are going to see. I believe that we are right on the threshold of wonderful things, but I want to emphasize that all these things will be only through the power of the Holy Spirit. You must not think that these gifts will fall upon you like ripe cherries. There is a sense in which you have to pay the price for everything you get. We must earnestly desire God's best gifts and say "Amen" to any preparation the Lord takes us through. In this way, we will be humble, useable vessels through whom He Himself can operate by means of the Spirit's power.

16

The Gift of Prophecy

To another [is given] *prophecy.*
—1 Corinthians 12:10

I n the twelfth chapter of 1 Corinthians, the apostle Paul was writing about the diversities of the gifts given by the Spirit. We see the importance of the gift of prophecy from 1 Corinthians 14:1, where we are told to *"pursue love, and desire spiritual gifts, but especially that you may prophesy."* We also see that *"he who prophesies speaks edification and exhortation and comfort to men"* (v. 3). How important it is, then, that we should have this gift in manifestation in the church, so that believers might be built up and made strong and filled with the comfort of God. But with this, as with all other gifts, we should see that it is operated by the Spirit's power and brought forth in the anointing of the Spirit, so that everyone who hears prophecy—as it is brought forth by the Spirit of God—will know that it is truly God who is bringing forth what is for the edification of those who hear. It is the Spirit of God who takes of the *"deep things of God"* (1 Cor. 2:10) and reveals them, and anoints the prophet to give forth what is a revelation of the things of God.

Utterance in prophecy has a real lifting power and sheds real light on the truth to those who hear. Prophecy is never a reflection of our minds; it is something far deeper than this. By means of prophecy, we receive what is the mind of the Lord; and as we receive these blessed, fresh utterances through the Spirit of the Lord, the whole assembly is lifted into the realm of the spiritual. Our hearts and minds and whole bodies receive a quickening through the Spirit-given word. As the Spirit brings forth prophecy, we find there is healing, salvation, and power in every sentence. For this reason, it is one of the gifts that we ought to covet.

False versus True Prophecy

While we appreciate true prophecy, we must not forget that the Scriptures warn us in no uncertain terms concerning what is false. In 1 John 4:1, we are told, *"Beloved, do not believe every spirit, but test the spirits, whether they are of God; because many false prophets have gone out into the world."* John then went on to tell us how we can tell the difference between the true and the false:

> By this you know the Spirit of God: Every spirit that confesses that Jesus Christ has come in the flesh is of God, and every spirit that does not confess that Jesus Christ has come in the flesh is not of God. And this is the spirit of the Antichrist, which you have heard was coming, and is now already in the world.　　　　(1 John 4:2–3)

There are voices that seem like prophecy, and some believers have fallen into terrible darkness and bondage through listening to these counterfeits of the true gift of prophecy. True prophecy is always Christ-exalting, magnifying the Son of God, exalting the blood of Jesus Christ, encouraging believers to praise and worship the true God. False prophecy deals with things that do not edify and is designed to puff up its hearers and to lead them into error.

Many people picture the devil as a great, ugly monster with large ears, eyes, and a tail; but the Scriptures give us no such picture of him. He was a being of great beauty whose heart became lifted up against God. He is manifesting himself everywhere today as an *"angel of light"* (2 Cor. 11:14). He is full of pride, and if you aren't careful, he will try to make you think you are somebody. This is the weakness of most preachers and most men— the idea of being somebody! None of us are anything, and the more we know we are nothing, the more God can make us a channel of His power. May the dear Lord save us from continually being sidetracked by pride—it is the devil's trap. True prophecy will show you that Christ is *"all in all"* (Eph. 1:23), and that you are, in yourself, less than nothing and vanity. False prophecy will not magnify Christ, but will make you think that you are going to be someone great after all. You may be sure that such thoughts are inspired by "the chief of the sons of pride."

I want to warn you against the foolishness of continually seeking to hear "voices." Look in the Bible. There we have the voice of God, *"who at various times and in various ways spoke in time past to the fathers by the prophets,* [and] *has in these last days spoken to us by His Son"* (Heb. 1:1–2). Don't run away with anything else. If you hear the voice of God, it will be according to the Scriptures of Truth given in the inspired Word. In Revelation 22:18–19, we see the danger of attempting to add to or take from the prophecy of this Book. True prophecy, as it comes forth in the power of the Spirit of God, will neither take from nor add to the Scriptures, but will intensify and quicken what already has been given to us by God. The Holy Spirit will bring to our remembrance all the things that Jesus said and did (John 14:26). True prophecy will bring forth *"things new and old"* (Matt. 13:52) out of the Scriptures of Truth and will make them *"living and powerful"* (Heb. 4:12) to us.

Some may ask, "If we have the Scriptures, why do we need prophecy?" The Scriptures themselves answer this question. God has said that in the last days He will pour out His Spirit upon all flesh, and that *"your sons and your daughters shall prophesy"* (Acts 2:17). The Lord knew that, in these last days, prophecy would be a real means of blessing to us, and that is why we can count on Him to give us, by means of the Spirit, through His menservants and His maidservants, true prophetic messages (v. 18).

The Dangers of Listening to False Voices

Again, I want to warn you concerning listening to voices. I was at a meeting in Paisley, Scotland, and I came in touch with two young women. They were in a great state of excitement. These two girls were telegraph operators and were precious young women, having received the baptism in the Spirit. They were both longing to be missionaries. But whatever our spiritual state is, we are subject to temptations. An evil power came to one of these young women and said, "If you will obey me, I will make you one of the most wonderful missionaries who ever went out to the mission field." This was just the devil or one of his agents acting as an angel of light. The young woman was captured immediately by this suggestion, and she became so excited that her sister saw there was something wrong and asked their work supervisor if they could be excused for a while.

As the sister took her into a room, the power of the devil, endeavoring to imitate the Spirit of God, manifested itself in a voice, and led this young woman to believe that the missionary enterprise would be unfolded that night, if she would obey. This evil spirit said, "Don't tell anybody but your sister." I think that everything of God can be told to everybody. If you cannot preach what you live, your life is wrong. If you are afraid of telling what you do in secret, some day it will be told from the housetops (Luke 12:3). Don't think you will get out of it. What is pure comes to the light. *"He who does the truth comes to the light, that his deeds may be clearly seen, that they have been done in God"* (John 3:21).

The evil power went on to say to this girl, "Go to the railroad station tonight, and there will be a train coming in at 7:32. After you buy a ticket for yourself and your sister, you will have sixpence left. You will find a woman in a railway carriage dressed as a nurse, and opposite her will be a gentleman who has all the money you need." The first thing came true. She bought the tickets and had just sixpence left. Next, the train came in at exactly 7:32. But the next thing did not come true. The two sisters ran from the front to the back of that railroad train before it moved out, and nothing turned out as they had been told. As soon as the train moved out, the same voice came and said, "Over on the other platform." All that night, until 9:30, these two young women were rushed from platform to platform. As soon as it was 9:30, this same evil power said, "Now that I know you will obey me, I will make you the greatest missionaries." It is always something big! They might have known it was all wrong. The evil power said, "This gentleman will take you to a certain bank at a certain corner in Glasgow, where he will deposit all that money for you." Banks are not open at that time of night in Glasgow. If she had gone to the street this evil spirit mentioned, there probably would not have been a bank there. All they needed was a little common sense, and they would have seen that it was not the Lord. If you have your heart open for this kind of voice, you will soon get into a trap. We must remember that there are many evil spirits in the world.

Were these sisters delivered? Yes, after terrible travail with God, they were perfectly delivered. Their eyes were opened to see that this thing was not of God but of the devil. These two sisters are now laboring for the Lord in China and doing a blessed work for Him. If you do get into error along these lines, praise God, there is a way out. I praise God that He will break us down until all pride leaves us. The worst pride we can have is the pride of self-exaltation.

Paul wrote, at the commandment of the Lord,

Let two or three prophets speak, and let the others judge. But if anything is revealed to another who sits by, let the first keep silent. For you can all prophesy one by one, that all may learn and all may be encouraged. (1 Cor. 14:29–31)

If you are not humble enough to allow your prophecy to be judged, it is as surely wrong as you are wrong. Prophecy has to be judged. A meeting such as this one that Paul suggested would certainly be the greatest meeting you ever held. Praise God, the tide will rise to this. It will all come into perfect order when the church is bathed and lost in the great ideal of glorifying Jesus alone. Then things will come to pass that will be worthwhile.

Coupled with prophecy, you should see manifested the fruit of the Spirit that is goodness (Gal. 5:22). It was holy men who spoke in prophecy in days of old as the Holy Spirit prompted them (2 Pet. 1:21); and so, today, the prophet who can be trusted is a man who is full of goodness, the goodness that is the fruit of the Spirit. But when he gets out of this position and rests on his own individuality, he is in danger of being puffed up and becoming an instrument for the enemy.

I knew some people who had a wonderful farm; it was very productive and was in a very good neighborhood. They listened to voices telling them to sell everything and go to Africa. These voices had so unhinged them that they had scarcely had time to sell out. They sold their property at a ridiculous price. The same voice told them of a certain ship they were to sail on. When they got to the port, they found there wasn't a ship of that name.

The difficulty was to get them not to believe these false voices. They said perhaps it was the mind of the Lord to give them another ship, and the voice soon gave them the name of another ship. When they reached Africa, they didn't know any language that was spoken there. But the voice did not let them stop. They eventually came back brokenhearted, shaken through, and having lost all confidence in everything. If these people had had the sense to go to some men of God who were filled with the Spirit and seek their counsel, they would soon have been persuaded that these voices were not of God. But listening to these voices always brings about a spiritual pride that makes people think that they are superior to their fellow believers, and that they are above taking the counsel of men whom they think are not as filled with the Spirit as they are. If you hear any voices that make you think that you are superior to those whom God has put in the church to rule the church, watch out, for that is surely the devil.

We read in Revelation 19:10 that *"the testimony of Jesus is the spirit of prophecy."* You will find that true prophetic utterance always exalts the Lamb of God.

Fire and Faith

No prophetic touch is of any use unless there is fire in it. I never expect to be used by God until the fire burns. I feel that if I ever speak, it must be by the Spirit. At the same time, remember that the prophet must prophecy according to the measure of his faith (Rom. 12:6). If you rise up in your weakness, but also in love because you want to honor God, and you just begin, you will find the presence of the Lord upon you. Act in faith, and the Lord will meet you.

May God take us on and on into this glorious fact of faith, so that we may be so in the Holy Spirit that God will work through us along the lines of the miraculous and along the lines of prophecy. When we are operating in the Spirit, we will always know that it is no longer we but He who is working through us, bringing forth what is in His own divine good pleasure (Phil. 2:13).

17

The Discerning of Spirits

To another [is given] *discerning of spirits.*
—1 Corinthians 12:10

There is a vast difference between natural discernment and spiritual discernment. When it come to natural discernment, you will find that many people are loaded with it, and they can see so many faults in others. To such the words of Christ surely apply, *"Why do you look at the speck in your brother's eye, but do not perceive the plank in your own eye?"* (Luke 6:41). If you want to manifest natural discernment, focus the same on yourself for at least twelve months, and you will see so many faults in yourself that you will never want to fuss about the faults of another.

In the sixth chapter of Isaiah, we read of the prophet being in the presence of God. He found that even his lips were unclean, that everything was unclean (Isa. 6:5). But praise God, there is the same live coal for us today (vv. 6–7), the baptism of fire, the perfecting of the heart, the purifying of the mind, the regeneration of the spirit. How important it is that the fire of God touches our tongues!

Discerning Spirits

In 1 John 4:1 we are told, *"Beloved, do not believe every spirit, but test the spirits, whether they are of God."* We are further told:

> And every spirit that does not confess that Jesus Christ has come in the flesh is not of God. And this is the spirit of the Antichrist, which you have heard was coming, and is now already in the world. (1 John 4:3)

From time to time, as I have seen a person under the power of evil or having a fit, I have said to the power of evil or satanic force that is within the possessed person, "Did Jesus Christ come in the flesh?" and right away they have answered no. They either say no or hold their tongues, refusing altogether to acknowledge that the Lord Jesus Christ came in the flesh. It is at a time like this when, remembering that further statement of John's, *"He who is in you is greater than he who is in the world"* (1 John 4:4), you can, in the name of the Lord Jesus Christ, deal with the evil powers and command them to come out. We, as Pentecostal people, must know the tactics of the evil one, and we must be able to displace and dislodge him from his position.

One time in Doncaster, England, I was preaching on the topic of faith, and a number of people were delivered. There was a man named Jack present who was greatly interested and moved by what he saw. He himself was suffering with a stiff knee and had yards and yards of flannel wound around it. After he got home, he said to his wife, "I have taken in Wigglesworth's message, and now I am going to act on it and get deliverance.

Wife, I want you to be the audience." He took hold of his knee and said, "Come out, devil, in the name of Jesus." Then he said, "It is all right, wife." He took the yards of flannel off and found he was all right without the bandage.

The next night he went to the little Primitive Methodist church where he worshipped. There were a lot of young people there who were in bad situations, and Jack had a tremendous ministry delivering his friends through the name of Jesus. He had been given to see that a great many ills to which flesh is heir are nothing else but the operation of the enemy; but his faith had risen, and he saw that in the name of Jesus there was a power that was more than a match for the enemy.

I arrived one night at Gottenberg in Sweden and was asked to hold a meeting there. In the midst of the meeting, a man fell full length in the doorway. The evil spirit threw him down, manifesting itself and disturbing the whole meeting. I rushed to the door and laid hold of this man and cried out to the evil spirit within him, "Come out, you devil! In the name of Jesus, we cast you out as an evil spirit." I lifted him up and said, "Stand on your feet and walk in the name of Jesus." I don't know whether anybody in the meeting understood me except the interpreter, but the devils knew what I said. I spoke in English, but these demons in Sweden cleared out. A similar thing happened in Oslo, Norway.

Satan will always endeavor to fascinate people through the eyes and through the mind. One time there was brought to me a beautiful young woman who had been obsessively fascinated with some preacher; just because he had not given her satisfaction on the lines of courtship and marriage, the devil had taken advantage of the situation and had made her delirious and insane.

Concerned friends had brought her two hundred and fifty miles in that condition. She had previously received the baptism in the Spirit.

You ask, "Is there any place for the enemy in one who has been baptized in the Holy Spirit?" Our only safety is in going on with God and in constantly being filled with the Holy Spirit. You must not forget Demas. He must have been baptized with the Holy Spirit, for he appears to have been one of Paul's right-hand workers, but the enemy got him to the place where he loved this present world, and he fell away (2 Tim. 4:10).

When they brought this young woman to me, I discerned the evil power right away and immediately cast the thing out in the name of Jesus. It was a great joy to present her before all the people in her right mind again.

There is a life of perfect deliverance, and this is where God wants you to be. If I find that my peace is disturbed in any way, I know it is the enemy who is trying to work. How do I know this? Because the Lord has promised to keep your mind in perfect peace when it is focused on Him (Isaiah 26:3). Paul told us to present our bodies as *"a living sacrifice, holy, acceptable to God, which is* [our] *reasonable service"* (Rom. 12:1). The Holy Spirit also spoke this word through Paul:

> *And do not be conformed to this world, but be* **transformed by the renewing of your mind***, that you may prove what is that good and acceptable and perfect will of God.*
> (Rom. 12:2, emphasis added)

Paul further told us,

> *Finally, brethren, whatever things are true, whatever things are noble, whatever things are just,*

*whatever things are pure, whatever things are
lovely, whatever things are of good report, if there
is any virtue and if there is anything praiseworthy;
meditate on these things.* (Phil. 4:8)

As we think about what is pure, we become pure. As
we think about what is holy, we become holy. And as we
think about our Lord Jesus Christ, we become like Him.
We are changed into the likeness of the object on which
our gaze is fixed.

How to Discern Spirits

To discern spirits, we must dwell with Him who is
holy, and He will give the revelation and unveil the mask
of satanic power in all its forms. In Australia, I went to
one place where there were disrupted and broken
homes. The people were so deluded by the evil power of
the devil that men had left their wives, and wives had left
their husbands, and had gotten into spiritual affinity with
one another. That is the devil! May God deliver us from
such evils in these days. There is no one better than the
companion God has given you. I have seen so many
broken hearts and so many homes that have been
wrecked. We need a real revelation of these evil seduc-
ing spirits that come in and fascinate by the eye and destroy lives, and bring the work of God into disrepute. But
there is always flesh behind it. It is never clean; it is un-
holy, impure, satanic, devilish; hell is behind it. If the enemy comes in to tempt you along these lines, I implore
you to look instantly to the Lord Jesus. He can deliver
you from any such satanic power. You must be separated from evil and separated unto God in all ways if you
are going to have faith.

The Holy Spirit will give us this gift of discerning of spirits if we desire it so that we may perceive by revelation this evil power that comes in to destroy. We can reach out and get this anointing of the Spirit that will reveal these things to us.

Sometimes spiritualists will come to your prayer meetings. You must be able to deal with spiritistic conditions. You can deal with them in such a way that they will not have any power in the meetings. If you ever have Theosophists or Christian Scientists in your meetings, you must be able to discern them and keep them under control. Never play with them; always clear them out. They are always better with their own company, unless they are willing to be delivered from the delusion they are in. Remember the warning of the Lord Jesus, *"The thief does not come except to steal, and to kill, and to destroy"* (John 10:10).

Hindrances to Discernment

Before the devil can bring his evil spirits, there has to be an open door. Hear what the Scriptures say: *"The wicked one does not touch him"* (1 John 5:18), and *"The LORD shall preserve you from all evil; He shall preserve your soul"* (Ps. 121:7). How does the devil get an opening? When the believer ceases to seek holiness, purity, righteousness, truth; when he ceases to pray, stops reading the Word, and gives way to carnal appetites. Then it is that the enemy comes. So often sickness comes as a result of disobedience. David said, *"Before I was afflicted I went astray"* (Ps. 119:67).

Seek the Lord, and He will sanctify every thought, every act, until your whole being is ablaze with holy purity, and your one desire will be for Him who has created you in holiness. Oh, this holiness! Can we be made pure? We can. Every inbred sin must go. God can cleanse away every evil thought. Can we have a hatred for sin and a love for righteousness? Yes, God will create within you a pure heart. He will *"take the heart of stone out of your flesh and give you a heart of flesh"* (Ezek. 36:26). He will sprinkle you with clean water and you will be cleansed from all your filthiness (v. 25). When will He do this? When You seek Him for such inward purity.

18

The Gift of Tongues

*Pursue love, and desire spiritual gifts, but especially that
you may prophesy. For he who speaks in a ["an unknown,"
KJV] tongue does not speak to men but to God,
for no one understands him; however,
in the spirit he speaks mysteries.*
—1 Corinthians 14:1–2

I t is necessary that we have a great desire for spiritual
gifts. We must thirst after them and covet them earnestly because the gifts are necessary and important,
and so that we, having received the gifts by the grace of
God, may be used for God's glory.

Tongues Are for Intercession

God has ordained this speaking in an unknown
tongue to Himself as a wonderful, supernatural means of
communication in the Spirit. As we speak to Him in an
unknown tongue, we speak wonderful mysteries in the
Spirit. In Romans 8:27, we read, *"He who searches the
hearts knows what the mind of the Spirit is, because He
makes intercession for the saints according to the will of
God."* Many times, as we speak to God in an unknown

209

tongue, we are in intercession; and as we pray thus in the Spirit, we pray according to the will of God. And there is such a thing as the Spirit making intercession *"with groanings which cannot be uttered"* (v. 26).

Along these lines, I want to tell you about Willie Burton, who is laboring for God in the Belgian Congo (Zaire). Brother Burton is a mighty man of God and is giving his life for the heathen in Africa. At one point, he took fever and went down to death. Those who ministered with him said, "He has preached his last. What shall we do?" All their hopes seemed to be blighted, and there they stood, with broken hearts, wondering what was going to take place. They had left him for dead; however, in a moment, without any signal, he stood right in the midst of them, and they could not understand it. The explanation he gave was that when he came to himself, he felt a warmth going right through his body, and there wasn't one thing wrong with him.

How did this happen? It was a mystery until he went to London and was telling the people how he had been left for dead and then was miraculously raised up. A lady came up and asked for a private conversation with him, and they arranged a time to meet. When they met together, she asked, "Do you keep a diary?"

He answered, "Yes."

Then she told him, "It happened that, on a certain day, I went to pray; and as soon as I knelt, I had you on my mind. The Spirit of the Lord took hold of me and prayed through me in an unknown tongue. A vision came before me in which I saw you lying helpless; and I cried out in the unknown tongue until I saw you rise up and go out of that room." She had kept a note of the time, and when he looked in his diary, he found that it was exactly the time when he was raised up.

The Gift of Tongues

There are great possibilities as we yield to the Spirit and speak to God in quiet hours in our bedrooms. God wants you to be filled with the Holy Spirit so that everything about you will be charged with the dynamite of heaven.

Tongues Are for Personal Edification

"He who speaks in a tongue edifies himself, but he who prophesies edifies the church" (1 Cor. 14:4). I want you to see that he who speaks in an unknown tongue edifies himself, or builds himself up. We must be edified before we can edify the church.

I cannot estimate what I, personally, owe to the Holy Spirit method of spiritual edification. I am here before you as one of the biggest conundrums in the world. There never was a weaker man on the platform. Did I have the capacity to speak? Not at all. I was full of inability. All natural things in my life point to exactly the opposite of my being able to stand on the platform and preach the Gospel.

The secret is that the Holy Spirit came and brought this wonderful edification of the Spirit. I had been reading the Word continually as well as I could, but the Holy Spirit came in and took hold of it, because the Holy Spirit is the breath of it, and He illuminated it to me. He gives me a spiritual language that I cannot speak fast enough—it comes too fast—and it is there because God has given it.

When the Comforter, or Helper, comes, *"He will teach you **all** things"* (John 14:26, emphasis added). He has given me this supernatural means of speaking in an unknown tongue to edify myself, so that, after being edified, I can edify the church.

211

EVER INCREASING FAITH

The Anointing Remains in You

In 1 John 2:20, we read, *"But you have an anointing from the Holy One, and you know all things."* Then, in verse 27, we read,

> But the anointing which you have received from Him abides in you, and you do not need that anyone teach you; but as the same anointing teaches you concerning all things, and is true, and is not a lie, and just as it has taught you, you will abide in Him. (1 John 2:27)

Even when you are baptized in the Spirit, you may say, "I seem so dry; I don't know where I am." The Word says you have an anointing. Thank God you have received an anointing.

In the above passage from 1 John, the Holy Spirit says that He *"abides"* and that He *"teaches you concerning all things."* These are great and definite positions for you.

The Holy Spirit wants you to stir up your faith to believe that this word is true—that you have the anointing and that the anointing abides. As you rise up in the morning, believe this wonderful truth; and as you yield to the Spirit's presence and power, you will find yourself speaking to God in the Spirit, and you will find that you are personally being edified by doing this.

Let everything about you be a lie, but let this word of God be true. Satan will say that you are the driest person and that you will never do anything; but believe God's promise to you, that *"the anointing which you have received from Him abides in you."*

The Gift of Tongues

Prophecy and the Interpretation of Tongues

I wish you all spoke with tongues, but even more that you prophesied; for he who prophesies is greater than he who speaks with tongues, unless indeed he interprets, that the church may receive edification. (1 Cor. 14:5)

You must understand that God wants you to be continually in the place of prophecy, for everyone who has received the Holy Spirit has a right to prophesy. In 1 Corinthians 14:31, we read, *"You can all prophesy one by one."* Now prophecy is far in advance of speaking in tongues, except when you have the interpretation of the speaking in tongues, and then God gives an equivalent to prophecy. In verse 13, we read, *"Let him who speaks in a tongue pray that he may interpret."* This is an important word.

Two Types of Tongues

After I received the baptism in the Holy Spirit and spoke in tongues as the Spirit gave me utterance (Acts 2:4), I did not speak in tongues again for nine months. I was troubled about it because I went everywhere, laying hands upon people so that they might receive the Holy Spirit, and they were speaking in tongues, but I did not have the joy of speaking in them myself. God wanted to show me that the speaking in tongues as the Spirit gave utterance, which I received when I received the baptism, was distinct from the gift of tongues that I subsequently received. When I laid hands on other people and they received the Holy Spirit, I used to think, "Oh, Lord Jesus, it would be nice if You would let me speak in tongues." He withheld the gift from me, because He knew that I would meet many who would say that the baptism of the Holy Spirit can be received without the speaking in tongues, and that people simply received the gift of tongues when they received the baptism.

I did not receive the gift of tongues when I received the baptism; however, nine months later, I was going out the door one morning, speaking to the Lord in my own heart, when a flood of tongues poured forth from me. When the tongues stopped, I said to the Lord, "Now, Lord, I did not do it, and I wasn't seeking it; therefore, You have done it, and I am not going to move from this place until you give me the interpretation." And then came an interpretation that has been fulfilled all over the world. Is it not the Holy Spirit who speaks? Then the Holy Spirit can interpret. Let him who speaks in a tongue ask for the interpretation, and God will give it. We must not rush through without getting a clear understanding of what God has to say to us.

Praying with the Spirit and with the Understanding

"What is the conclusion then? I will pray with the spirit, and I will also pray with the understanding. I will sing with the spirit, and I will also sing with the understanding" (1 Cor. 14:15). If you pray in an unknown tongue in the Spirit, you do not know what you are praying; you have no understanding of it; it is unfruitful to those around you. But you have the same power to pray with the understanding under the anointing of the Spirit as you have to pray in an unknown tongue.

Some say, "Oh, I could do that, but it would be myself doing it." If *you* pray, it is yourself, and everything you do in the beginning is yourself. When I kneel down to pray, the first and second sentences may be in the natural; but as soon as I have finished, the Spirit begins to pray through me. Granted, the first may be yourself. The next will be the Holy Spirit, and the Holy Spirit will take you through, praise the Lord.

Everything but faith will say, "That isn't right."

Faith says, "It is right."

The natural man says, "It isn't right."

Faith says, "It is right."

Paul said, *"I will pray with the spirit, and I will also pray with the understanding"* (1 Cor. 14:15), and he did it in faith.

Satan is against it, and your own self-life is against it. May God the Holy Spirit bring us into that blessed place where we may live, walk, pray, and sing in the Spirit, and pray and sing with the understanding, also. Faith will do it.

Faith has a deaf ear to the devil and to the working of the natural mind, and a big ear to God. Faith has a deaf ear to your self and an open ear to God. Faith won't take any notice of your feelings.

Faith declares, *"You are complete in Him"* (Col. 2:10).

It is a wonderful thing to pray in the Spirit and to sing in the Spirit—praying in tongues and singing in tongues as the Spirit of God gives you utterance. I never get out of bed in the morning without having communion with God in the Spirit. It is the most wonderful thing on earth. It is most lovely to be in the Spirit when you are getting dressed, and then when you come out into the world, to find that the world has no effect on you. If you begin the day like that, you will be conscious of the guidance of the Spirit all during the day.

Tongues Should Be Spoken in an Orderly Way

I thank my God I speak with tongues more than you all; yet in the church I would rather speak five words with my understanding, that I may teach others also, than ten thousand words in a ["an unknown," KJV] tongue. (1 Cor. 14:18–19)

Many people will come to you and declare that Paul said he would rather speak five words with the known tongue than ten thousand words without understanding. They will always leave out the part of the passage that reads, *"I thank my God I speak with tongues more than you all"* (1 Cor. 14:18). In this passage, Paul was correcting the practice of excessive speaking in tongues without interpretation, which would not edify the assembly. If there was no one with the gift of interpretation present, the people were simply to speak to themselves and to God.

Suppose someone were preaching and twenty or thirty people stood up in succession to speak in tongues. It would be a very serious problem. There would be confusion. The people attending the meeting would rather have five words of edification, consolation, and comfort (1 Cor. 14:3) than ten thousand words without understanding.

Just because you feel a touch of the Spirit, you are not obligated to speak in tongues. The Lord will give you a sound mind (2 Tim. 1:7), so that you will hold your body in perfect order for the edification of the church. But in 1 Corinthians 14:18, Paul said that he spoke in tongues more than all of the Corinthians; and, as it is evident that the Corinthian church was very considerably given to speaking in tongues, he certainly must have been speaking in tongues a great amount both day and night. He was so edified by this wonderful, supernatural means of being built up, that he could go to the church and preach in a manner in which they could all understand him, and could marvelously edify the believers.

Tongues Are for Unbelievers

In the law it is written: "With men of other tongues and other lips I will speak to this people; And yet, for all that, they will not hear Me," says the Lord. Therefore tongues are for a sign, not to those who believe but to unbelievers.
(1 Cor. 14:21–22)

There are many who call themselves believers who are extremely unbelieving. One such unbelieving "believer" was a Methodist minister who lived in Sheffield, England. A man gave him a check and told him to use the money to go and take a rest. This man also gave him my name and address. Hence, when the minister arrived in Bradford, he began to inquire about me. He was warned against me as one of the "tongues people," and was told to be very careful not to be taken in, for the whole thing was of the devil. He said, "They will not take *me* in. I know too much for them to take me in."

He was quite run down and needed rest. When he arrived at my house, he said, "A friend of yours sent me. Is it all right?"

I replied, "Yes, you are welcome."

But we could do nothing with that man. It was impossible. You never heard anyone talk like he did. All he did was talk, talk, talk, talk.

I said, "Let him alone; he will surely finish some day." We had dinner, and he talked through dinnertime. We had the next meal, and he talked through that.

That evening we held our Friday night meeting for those seeking the baptism in the Holy Spirit, and the room began to fill with people, but still he talked. No one could get a word in edgewise. He lodged himself in a place where he could not be disturbed by those coming in.

Finally, I said, "Brother, you will have to stop now; we are going to pray."

Generally, we had some singing before going to prayer, but this time it was different. It was God's order. We got straight to prayer, and as soon as we began to pray, two young women, one on one side and the other on the other side, began speaking in tongues. This minister—it was all so strange to him—moved from one to the other to hear what they were saying.

In a little while, he said, "May I go to my room?"

I said, "Yes, brother, if you wish." So he went to his room, and we had a wonderful time at the meeting.

We went to bed about eleven o'clock or so, and at half-past three in the morning, this man came to my bedroom door. He knocked on the door and said, "May I come in?"

"Yes, come in," I said.

He opened the door and said, "He is come; He is come." As he spoke, he held his mouth, for he could hardly speak in English.

I said, "Go back to bed, and tell us tomorrow."

Tongues are for the unbeliever (1 Cor. 14:22), and this man was an unbeliever, an unbelieving "believer." Again and again, I have seen conviction come upon people through the speaking in tongues.

The Gift of Tongues

The next morning, this man came down to breakfast and said, "Oh, wasn't that a wonderful night? I know Greek and Hebrew, and those two young women were speaking these languages. One was saying in Greek, 'Get right with God,' and the other was saying the same thing in Hebrew. I knew it was God, and not they, who was speaking. I first had to repent. I came in an unbeliever, but I found that God was here. In the night, God laid me on the floor for about two hours. I was helpless. Then God broke through." And at that moment he began to speak in tongues again, right at the breakfast table.

God will have witnesses of His mighty power that no man can deny. You will have to see that the Holy Spirit will speak through you in tongues and interpretation that will bring conviction to the unbeliever, and you will find that God will convict by this means.

Seek God's Best with All Your Heart

I will explain to you the most perfect way to receive the gift. Come with me to the second chapter of 2 Kings, and I will show you a man receiving a gift. The prophet Elijah had been mightily used by God in calling down fire and in other miracles. Elisha, his chosen successor, was moved with a great spirit of covetousness to have this man's gifts. You can be very covetous for the gifts of the Spirit and God will allow it. When Elijah said to him, "I want you to stay at Gilgal," Elisha said, *"As the LORD lives, and as your soul lives, I will not leave you!"* (See 2 Kings 2:1–2.) There was no stopping him.

Likewise, when Elijah wanted Elisha to stay at Jericho, he said, in essence, "I am not stopping." The man who stops gets nothing. Oh, don't stop at Jericho; don't stop at Jordan; don't stop anywhere when God wants

219

you to move on into all of His fullness that He has for you.

Elijah and Elisha came to the Jordan River, and Elijah took his mantle and struck the waters. The waters divided, and Elijah and Elisha went across on dry ground. Elijah turned to Elisha and said, in essence, "Look here, what do you want?" Elisha wanted what he was going to have, and you may covet all that God says that you shall have. Elisha said, *"Please let a double portion of your spirit be upon me"* (2 Kings 2:9). This was the plowboy who had washed the hands of his master (1 Kings 19:19–20; 2 Kings 3:11); but his spirit got so big that he purposed in his heart that, when Elijah stepped off the scene, he would be put into his place.

Elijah said, *"You have asked a hard thing. Nevertheless, if you see me when I am taken from you, it shall be so for you"* (2 Kings 2:10). May God help you never to stop persevering until you get what you want. Let your aspiration be large and your faith rise until you are wholly on fire for God's best.

Onward they went, and as one stepped, the other stepped with him. Elisha purposed to keep his eyes on his master until the last. It took a chariot of fire and horses of fire to separate them, and Elijah went up by a whirlwind into heaven. I can imagine Elisha crying out, "Father Elijah, drop that mantle!" And it came down. Oh, I can see it lowering and lowering and lowering. Elisha took all of his own clothes and tore them in two pieces, and then he took up the mantle of Elijah. (See vv. 11–13.) I do not believe that, when he put on that other mantle, he felt any different in himself; but when he came to the Jordan, he took the mantle of Elijah, struck the waters, and said, *"Where is the LORD God of Elijah?"* (v. 14). The waters parted, and he went over on dry ground. And the sons of the prophets said, *"The spirit of Elijah rests on Elisha"* (v. 15).

It is like receiving a gift; you don't know that you have it until you act in faith. Brothers and sisters, as you ask, *believe.*

ANOTHER POWERFUL *B*OOK

from Whitaker House

Smith Wigglesworth Devotional
Smith Wigglesworth
ISBN: 0-88368-574-4
Trade • 558 pages

Answering God's call, Smith Wigglesworth took God at His word with dramatic results. Sight was restored to the blind, hearing to the deaf, health to the diseased, and mental wholeness to the insane. Even some who were dead were brought back to life. Your faith will expand as you read Wigglesworth's challenging insights into faith-filled living. As you daily explore these truths from the Apostle of Faith, you will connect with God's glorious power, cast out doubt, build up your faith, and see impossibilities turn into realities. Your prayer life will be transformed as you experience the joy of seeing powerful results when you minister to others.

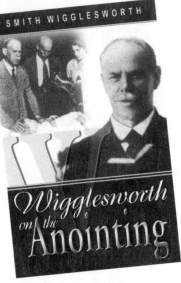